DAY CARE DECEPTION

DAY CARE DECEPTION

WHAT THE CHILD CARE
ESTABLISHMENT ISN'T TELLING US

BRIAN C. ROBERTSON

ENCOUNTER BOOKS
SAN FRANCISCO

First edition published in 2003 by Encounter Books, an activity of Encounter for Culture and Education, Inc., a nonprofit tax exempt corporation.

Encounter Books website address: www.encounterbooks.com
Manufactured in the United States and printed on acid-free paper.

The paper used in this publication meets the minimum requirements of ANSI/NISO Z39.48-1992 (R 1997)(*Permanence of Paper*).

Library of Congress Cataloging-in-Publication Data

Robertson, Brian C., 1964–
    Day care deception : what the child care establishment isn't telling us / Brian C. Robertson.
    p. cm.
    Includes bibliographical references and index.
    ISBN 1-893554-67-8
    1. Child care—United States—Evaluation.   2. Day care centers—United States.   3. Child care services—Government policy—United States.   4. Family policy—Political aspects—United States.   5. Child development—United States.   6. Work and family—Unites States.   7. United States—social conditions—1945–.   I. Title: Day care deception : what the child care establishment isn't telling us.   II. Title.
    HQ778.63.R623 2003
    362.71'2'0973—dc21

                    2003049138

10 9 8 7 6 5 4 3 2 1

To all the parents who put their children first,
in spite of everything.

Contents

Introduction

The question of widespread use of day care for preschool children is not your typical liberal versus conservative issue. What social critic David Gelernter terms the "Motherhood Revolution" has affected us all, the Red America from the TV election maps of 2000 and also the Blue. In the quarter-century between 1970 and 1995, the proportion of married women with children under six years of age in the labor force rose from 30 percent to 64 percent (it has not changed substantially since then), necessitating dramatic alterations in the care arrangements made for preschool children. As Gelernter notes, there are a wide variety of causes behind this Motherhood Revolution, both cultural and economic.[1] Many of these—radical feminism, the financial pressures pushing married couples toward the dual-income family model, the elimination of the social supports that undergird the rearing of children—are addressed in the chapters that follow.

But in addition to these cultural and financial factors, there may be another, more subtle force at play in the decision of married mothers to work during their children's preschool years. Since just after the Second World War, parents have felt increasingly marginalized by educational and psychiatric "experts" in the whole project of raisng their children. As theories about proper intellectual and psychological stimulation for young children have multiplied—and become

1

increasingly contradictory—parents, particularly mothers, have been intimidated into surrendering a good deal of their natural prerogatives as the primary educators of their children to a professional class of child care experts. In her influential book *The Feminine Mystique,* Betty Friedan described the suburban housewife's existence as one of spirit-killing boredom in mundane and repetitive chores; but much of that domestic ennui was actually just as much a result of the slow, steady erosion of mothers' confidence in their role in the formation of their own children. Combined with the encroaching isolation of mothers at home in a society where almost all other adults have full professional lives, this diminution of parental autonomy has played a large role in the devaluation of motherhood—almost as large as the unremitting hostility of the popular culture to traditional conceptions of the family, derided as "Ozzie and Harriet" mythology.

One of my intentions in writing this book is to make the case that deference to the "experts" regarding the care of young children is unwise, and has proved detrimental to the interests of children and parents alike. While theories about the conditions under which children thrive have changed dramatically over the years, one fundamental fact has remained stubbornly constant in the sociological research: a child's development depends crucially on the amount of attention he or she gets from parents during the first three or four years of life. Parents are the most reliable "child development experts" for the simple reason that they know the needs of their own children better than anyone else. Theories of development, often colored by ideological positions on the family and its role in society, should take a back seat to the actual experience of parenting and the instinctive understanding that parents have about what rearing children requires. Parenting is for parents, not child development experts or day care "professionals."

Another reason for writing this book is my desire that public policy in the area of child care be more reflective of, and responsive to, the wishes of parents. While I believe there are conclusive arguments for ending the grossly inequitable system that subsidizes the choice for commercial day care at the expense of parents who care for their children at home, it must be acknowledged that some parents in difficult circumstances—particularly single mothers—have no choice but to use commercial day care services. Some parents, and their children, will require such alternatives to parental care when less formal arrangements, such as care by relatives, are not available. But policymakers who wish to be compassionate toward these parents should think twice about making policy based on the hard cases. As in other areas of public policy, the history of child care policy in the United States demonstrates how turning the undesirable, abnormal situation into the guiding standard has the effect of damaging the very institutions that, *in extremis,* it seeks to replace. When government gets into the business of child care, it necessarily undermines the family. In the cause of supporting at-risk or stressed families, government inevitably undermines healthy ones.

THE INVOLVEMENT OF GOVERNMENT in the care of preschoolers dates back to the Lanham Act of 1941, which provided funds for the construction and operation of day care centers for the children of female defense workers. A temporary measure to deal with the contingencies of war, it expired in 1945. Interestingly, though, it highlighted a rift among policymakers that foreshadowed a major philosophical change in notions of proper childrearing. "Maternalist" feminists in the first half of the century had been largely responsible for the institution of measures such as Aid to Dependent Children (ADC) precisely with the purpose of insuring "full-time maternal care in the home" for children whose fathers were unable to support the family due to death, incapacity or simple dereliction. Proponents of ADC argued that mothers should not be forced to work out of economic necessity, nor should poverty "deprive a child of the full-time care of his or her mother." But the maternalist feminists at the U.S. Children's Bureau began to encounter ideological opposition within the federal bureaucracy—notably at the Women's Bureau, where the idea of government-subsidized day care was beginning to be viewed more favorably. Children's Bureau head Martha Wood expressed her opposition to the idea of extending the day care subsidies in 1945, saying that while "the Children's Bureau would not want to make a statement that mothers should remain in their homes ... we do know that children are affected by the mother's absence for the long day."[2]

Ironically, it was growing concern over a burgeoning welfare culture, already taking root in the pre–Great Society days of the early 1960s, that occasioned the first effective peacetime push for day care subsidies. Advocates of a federal day care program noted that the majority of ADC funds were going not to the widows they were designed to protect, but to unwed mothers, and thus helping to breed a culture of illegitimacy and welfare dependency in the inner cities. These reformers enacted new work requirements at the state level, which began to push poor mothers into the workforce. This went contrary to the traditional position of the Children's Bureau, as expressed by its former chief Katherine Lenroot, that ADC should "make it possible for a mother to remain at home if she sees fit to do so." But the new work requirements and public concern over the sloth of ADC recipients gave an opening to the new "child welfare advocates," who used ADC reform as a means to move in the direction of a national day care program. In 1962, Congress passed day care funding for those poor mothers expected to enter the workforce and leave the care of their children to others. As one historian writes, it was "a neat turn of policy rhetoric" that allowed child welfare advocates "to use the crisis over welfare to reinvent publicly funded day care. What many Americans had previously seen as a threat to traditional family life was now offered as its savior. The true threats to families were welfare dependency, illegitimacy, absent fathers, and idleness"—and day care was held up as a solution, not part of a larger picture of family breakdown. The maternalist feminists would have been appalled.[3]

Another step along the road toward subsidizing a day care regime for preschoolers was Head Start, begun in the mid-1960s. Although it was conceived as a remedial program for children from underprivileged backgrounds, one of its important effects was to foster the gradual acceptance of government intervention in the care and education of preschool children. Today Head Start, widely assumed to be a success despite its failure to improve school performance measurably for poor children, receives over $6 billion a year.[4]

A more important impetus for more government involvement in the education and care of preschool children was the radical feminism of the late 1960s, which began to agitate for universal day care as a way of liberating women from the drudgery of the home. In policy terms, the radical feminist influence was first felt at the 1970 White House Conference on Children, whose policy conclusions differed dramatically from those of its predecessors. Previous gatherings of academics and business representatives had contended, with little or no evidence, that for mothers to be working outside the home did no harm to children; but the 1970 meeting was more politically charged. A significant contingent of feminist and civil rights activists was bent on overturning long-held assumptions about the family. While the conference report did not attack the traditional family per se, it signaled a fundamental policy shift in its completely relativistic views on the structure of domestic life. We "do not favor any particular family form," the delegates wrote. "Children can and do flourish under many other family forms than the traditional nuclear structure."[5]

Feminist delegates saw the White House Conference on Children as an ideal place to float the notion that professional day care was a perfectly adequate alternative to maternal care. In order to make the case that a mother who chooses to work outside the home is not irresponsible, they strove to undermine the traditional belief that children are best cared for at home. The conference report reflected this agenda: "The *place* where care is given is not the most significant dimension for the child. . . . The issue is the kind of care given, how this is handled, what abilities are nurtured, what values are learned, and what attitudes toward people are acquired."[6] The advantages that day care presented for the proper socialization of children were also emphasized. "Think for a moment what this would mean," said Representative Bella Abzug, a conference delegate. "It would let local groups of parents and women set up child care centers for children from all socioeconomic backgrounds. . . . A child care system that would accommodate rich and poor alike, that would let our kids grow up with a chance to know each other and to learn that they can bridge the racial and economic gap that divides their parents."[7]

Out of this atmosphere of social engineering came a recommendation "that [universal] federally supported public education be available for children at age three."[8] Estimating that the plan would cost "$75 to $100 billion a year," Professor Edward Zigler, one of the conference's architects, urged that the program "become part of the very structure of our society" and maintained that "the child care solution must cover the child from as early in pregnancy as possible through at least the first 12 years of life." He proposed a "partnership between parents and the children's caretakers" as the norm to be achieved.[9] The final report of the 1970 conference was perhaps more candid than Zigler about the intent of such a regime: "Day care is a powerful institution. A day care program that ministers to a child from six months to six years of age has over 8,000 hours to teach him values, fears, beliefs, and behaviors."[10]

It was, as the sociologists later said, a huge "paradigm shift." The very next year brought a tax reform that allowed significant deductions for parents using commercial day care, shifting tax incentives from the home toward nonparental care for the first time. Earlier in 1971, Congress had passed a much more radical day care measure, the Mondale-Brademas "Comprehensive Child Development" bill, which would have mandated attendance at federally run centers for almost every preschool child in the United States. But the bill was unexpectedly vetoed by President Richard Nixon, who noted in his veto message that the measure would have the effect of pledging "the vast moral authority of the federal government to the side of communal approaches to childrearing as against a family centered approach." Nixon accurately pronounced the bill "the most radical piece of legislation to emerge from the 92nd Congress."[11]

Even though such a radical system of universal day care for preschoolers was defeated, since Nixon's veto the trend in government child care policy has been moving slowly but surely toward more subsidization of "professional," nonparental care outside the home at the expense of care by parents in the home. The child care deduction was expanded in 1972, and then replaced by a more generous credit in 1976. In adding Title XX to the Social Security Act in 1974, Congress created a federal child care system that quickly came to embrace over one million children. In 1976 and again in 1984, Congress significantly increased and expanded tax preferences for child care outside the home. In 1981, it granted a special tax credit to two-income couples, specifically as a way to tax the domestic work of the mother and homemaker that evaded normal IRS measurements of income in the "productive" economy. This marked the first time that the federal government explicitly asserted the right to tax transactions in the domestic realm—the non-market economy of the home that the feminist maternalists had fought for so long to defend.[12]

Another attempt to introduce a universal program of preschool care was barely beaten back in 1990 when the Act for Better Child Care (ABC) died in the Senate after passing in the House. The $2.5 billion a year proposal called for expanded subsidies and heavy regulation of all child care, including care provided by grandmothers and family-based centers. Despite a highly orchestrated and effective publicity campaign calling attention to a supposed "child care crisis" among working parents, even supporters of the legislation admitted that there had been no groundswell of public sentiment for more federally supported day care. One of the bill's biggest proponents, Representative George Miller, later acknowledged with remarkable candor,

> I spent eight years in getting the child-care bill passed in Congress, and at its zenith, there was never a child-care movement in the country. There was a coalition of child-advocacy groups and a few large international unions that put in hundreds of thousands of dollars, and we created in the mind of the leadership of Congress that there was a child-care movement—but there was nobody riding me. And not one of my colleagues believed their election turned on it for a moment.[13]

Despite the narrow defeat of ABC, the day care establishment won a big victory with the inauguration of the Child Care and Development Block Grant and the At-Risk Child Care Program in 1990, a major expansion of the federal involvement in child care support.

Repesentative Miller's admission that the pro–day care lobby—the professional day care industry, big business interests and feminist groups—lacked any substantial grassroots support went generally unnoticed by Republicans, who had been extremely tentative in opposing the bill for fear of being branded reactionary opponents of working women. Another important factor in the GOP's unwillingness to make a political case against the growing regime of publicly subsidized day care is the fact that while the party's rank and file is opposed, the regime is popular among the party's corporate supporters. Ironically, the boldest and best way of warding off new initiatives for further subsidization of day care had been suggested two years earlier by George Bush, in a little-noticed proposal during the 1988 presidential campaign, which outgoing president Ronald Reagan referred to in a stump speech for Bush that year:

> The Vice President's plan would provide a refundable tax credit of $1,000 per child. Now, the basic idea here is that the Government would simply let families keep up to $1,000 more of their own money. That's money the family itself can decide on how to spend. Working mothers could put the money toward child care. But by giving each family this tax credit, the Vice President's plan would also permit thousands of mothers to choose to stay home with their children.[14]

Republicans, however, failed to recognize the broad political appeal of countering new initiatives for a government-subsidized day care system with options based on maximizing parental choice, and they quietly abandoned the idea until George W. Bush adopted a considerably scaled-down version as part of his tax reform package of 2001.

The political schizophrenia of conservatives on child care issues surfaced again in the mid-1990s with welfare reform. In a replay of the disputes of thirty years earlier, when day care advocates had capitalized on disapproval of the dependency culture bred by welfare, conservatives sided with day care advocates in imposing work requirements on welfare mothers and moving their children into day care. For years, welfare reform advocates had pointed out that nearly half of the recipients of Aid to Families with Dependent Children (AFDC) had been on the welfare rolls before, and they insisted that effective reform necessitated getting these women (most of them never-married mothers) off the dole and into the workplace. As a result, they looked favorably on proposals that combined job training and work requirements with funding for day care—even for mothers of preschoolers. Thus in 1988, conservatives provided important backing to the first "workfare" reforms, mandating that states "replace the existing AFDC program with a new Family Support Program which emphasizes work."[15]

Disappointed with the progress made in getting these welfare mothers off the rolls (largely due to the resistance of mothers to handing over their preschoolers to others), conservatives like Newt Gingrich were pushing even more radical versions of institutional childrearing. As the newly elected Speaker of the House of Representatives in December 1994, Gingrich and the new Republican majority pushed for dismantling the entire system of AFDC benefits, proposing that the children of parents not able to provide for them should be transferred to orphanages. As critic David Blankenhorn pointed out at the time, "The proposal to build more orphanages is similar to our current strategy of building more prisons. Both ideas assume that more brick-and-mortar structures, staffed by public or quasi-public employees can fill the vacuum in our society created by the growing collapse of parental capacity and the disintegration of the married-couple child-raising unit." The problem with the welfare culture, Blankenhorn pointed out, was not the nonworking mothers but the absence of working fathers. "As a national strategy for reversing the decline of child well-being, the fatherhood idea is far more consistent with the better angels of our nature than either the prison idea or the orphanage idea."[16]

As it happened, the welfare reform legislation passed by Congress and signed two years later by President Clinton (who had twice vetoed it) included no provisions for orphanages. But the pervasive philosophy of fiscal accountability and individual economic responsibility that guided Gingrich's ill-conceived proposal was still apparent in the measures that passed, with their focus on work requirements, child protection and day care funding. It was probably true, as conservatives argued, that AFDC payments were encouraging out-of-wedlock births among young, poor women. But as Wade Horn, then the director of the National Fatherhood Institute, pointed out, the problem was not only that AFDC served as social insurance for sexually irresponsible unmarried women, but that the payments were structured in a way that made marriage "an economically foolish choice" even for those in stable relationships. For most unmarried mothers receiving welfare at the time, marriage to a working father would mean a reduction of their *combined* income of anywhere between 20 and 30 percent.[17]

After five years of the new state-run welfare regime, the point remains valid. The vaunted "success" of welfare reform has consisted in a sharp reduction of the welfare rolls and a reduction of the number of children living in poor families, not in a lowering of illegitimacy rates or a strengthening of those poor families that have been undermined by perverse incentives and lack of opportunity. If policymakers had been more concerned with the family breakdown at the core of the welfare culture, they could have focused on job training and placement for fathers rather than for mothers of young children.

Rearranging the incentives by, for example, rewarding couples for marrying and staying married with preferences in assignment of public housing or by increasing the aid to *two-*

parent families would be a much more effective way of helping to restore the culture of marriage that itself is a major
promoter of responsibility and the ethic of work. After all,
in 20 percent of poor families both parents are present and
one is a full-time wage earner. Why not modestly subsidize
those families, who in effect are penalized under the current
system? The alternative is expending resources in an often-
futile effort to track down absent fathers and force them to
pay child support, while making huge outlays on day care
for mothers pushed into the workforce.[18] In the 1996 Welfare Reform Act, Congress provided a 50 percent increase in
day care funding to states, allowing them to use money freed
up by reductions in the welfare rolls for child care.

And how are the children of welfare reform faring? One
study of the day care provided in three states to the children
of mothers put to work by the reform measures of 1996 found
that the quality of the care was extremely poor. Children
spent hours on end watching television. Toddlers wandered
aimlessly without attention or interaction. Since the block
grant money is effectively barred from going to "religious"
day care providers, parental choice is restricted and the quality of care is lowered.[19] The authors of the study remarked
that in comparison with other national studies of day care
quality (which have also found care to be far from adequate),
the "children in the new welfare system have entered centers of even lower quality."[20] Little wonder that conscien-
tious mothers are reluctant to leave their children in such
facilities. One remarked to a reporter that she had "dropped
out of her job search to stay home with her five year old after
her daughter started talking about French-kissing boys and
going to a club 'to get a groove on with a man,' language
she picked up at a child care center."[21]

Overall, federal subsidies of the child care market have
increased in constant dollars from $2 million in 1965 to $15
billion in 2000, most of this in the form of block grants to

states.[22] In 2000, a U.S. Senate panel was shocked to learn how this block grant money was being used. An official of the Agriculture Department revealed that millions of dollars earmarked for providing day care for children of working poor were being spent on nonexistent services; some subsidized "day care centers" were actually empty lots or vacant buildings. Of the service actually provided, some was substandard to the point of criminality: in one case, investigators found twenty children in a windowless basement measuring ten feet by fifteen feet; in others, the facilities lacked basic safety equipment like smoke detectors and fire extinguishers. "It's absolutely incredible," Agriculture Department inspector general Roger Viadero said, telling a Senate subcommittee that frauds involving vacant day care centers were so common, "we get excited when we visit and find children there." One "day care provider" in Detroit collected $13 million by fabricating food bills for day care services never offered, spending some of the money on a Rolls Royce, more than twenty fur coats and lavish vacations before being convicted of fraud; another diverted $2.2 million to buy an extravagant house and pay for ski trips. The chief financial officer for the Agriculture Department acknowledged that the agency was having trouble determining where the federal funds earmarked for day care were going, admitting that they had lost track of $7.1 billion in funds.[23]

These stories of fraud and waste suggest that the much-publicized notion that poor mothers and "working families" are demanding the government to step in and support day care is largely a cover for increasing subsidies to the day care market in the form of the nonrefundable dependent-care tax credit, *most of which has not gone to poor families*. In 1994, only 13 percent of families claiming the credit had incomes of less than $20,000; 41 percent had incomes above $50,000.[24] While wealthy two-income parents purchasing child care can claim a net of $5,000 or more in federal tax benefits, low- or middle-income families struggling to give their own children full-time parental care get nothing; indeed, their taxes help support the day care used by the rich.

All this is necessary background for the continual reiteration of the notion that the supply of day care services is not keeping up with demand, thus justifying yet more government investment. The family breakdown that government policies have abetted feeds the "necessity" for more day care. Because of divorce and illegitimacy, well over half of all American children will spend all or part of their childhood with a single parent; it only stands to reason that the "need" for day care will grow until this trend is reversed.[25] Government policies have already contributed mightily to distorting the child care market, primarily by subsidizing center-based care at the expense of parents who want to care for their own children. This, in turn, boosts "demand" by making the decision to stay home with preschoolers or make informal arrangements for their care all the more difficult. Day care subsidies have not been driven by a grassroots demand among parents, but they have driven many of those parents into a financial position where resort to commercial day care seems like the only rational option.

In the pages that follow, I aim to provide the facts about day care— its institutional development and its human implications—that are essential to determining whether it really is a rational option for parents and children. I have written this book for parents seeking to make an informed choice for or against day care. It is a choice of great moment for them, their children, and the future of our nation.

ONE

A Lethal Reticence

n the spring of 1997, two years before she was murdered by Eric Harris and Dylan Klebold, Cassie Bernall made a dramatic turnaround. Her mother, Misty, had quit her job as a legal secretary the previous December in order to devote more time to Cassie and her younger brother, Chris, out of concern over their declining grades and Cassie's growing emotional distance from her and her husband, Brad.

Misty soon found out just how crucial that decision was. Looking for a book in her daughter's room, she ran across some letters written to Cassie by her closest friend at school, a girl Misty and Brad had always found a bit disturbing because of her sullen attitude and hostile manner. What Misty read was shocking. Amid adolescent chatter about sexual adventures and drug use, illustrated with drawings of occult symbols and daggers, the girl said this about a teacher: "Want to help me murder her? She called my parents and told them about my F." There followed a cartoon of the teacher lying in a pool of blood, with knives thrust into her chest. Another letter signed off, "Kill your parents! Murder is the answer to all of your problems. Make those scumbags pay for our suffering." Other drawings depicted the Bernalls stabbed to death and hanging by their entrails, as well as a knife dripping with "parents' guts" and tombstones inscribed "Ma and Pa Bernall, R.I.P." Yet another note, decorated with drawings of marijuana leaves and vampires, read, "My guts are hungry for that weird stuff. . . . I f—ing need to kill myself, we need to murder your parents. School is a f—ing bitch, kill me with your parents, then kill yourself so you don't go to jail." It later emerged that Cassie had written similar notes herself.

Misty and Brad took what some might consider drastic action in this age of unprecedented adolescent freedom, when many parents are fearful of intruding on their teenagers' autonomy. Despite their daughter's rage at what she regarded as an invasion of her privacy, they showed the letters found in Cassie's room to both the sheriff's office and the other girl's parents. They took Cassie out of public school and enrolled her in a private Christian school; they searched her room and backpack regularly; they monitored her use of the phone; they forbade her to leave the house without specific permission; and they immediately cut off her contact with her girlfriend (and anyone else in her old crowd of friends). The only activities Cassie was allowed to participate in were with her church youth group. The Bernalls moved to a new neighborhood, away from Cassie's old crowd. Misty stayed home so as to supervise her daughter more closely.

Aside from the financial pressures entailed in their decision to go from two incomes to one while paying the cost of private schooling, the Bernalls were also well aware that the course they had chosen might further alienate Cassie from them. Misty later wrote:

> In a way, it's the hardest thing you can ever do as parents: to put your foot down and say, "This stops right here." Not that we thought it would be easy. We knew we were risking an even bigger battle than the one set off by our discovery of the letters.

They realized, however, that the risk was even greater if they did not try to reestablish a relationship of trust and understanding. As Misty put it, Cassie's distance was the result of an enormous gulf of miscommunication and hostility between us—a gulf that only time, love, and attention would bridge.... I knew that if we were ever going to truly rebuild our relationship with Cassie, we ourselves had some work to do.... Like it or not, we had lost Cassie's trust and respect just as she had lost ours, and the route to regaining it would have to be a two-way street.[1]

In addition to their closer supervision of Cassie, Misty and Brad decided that a change in their philosophy of parenting was also in order. They realized that they had often been more interested in gaining Cassie's friendship than in earning her respect. Instead of attempting to win her over by pleasing her, they now put their efforts into providing Cassie with clearer guidelines.

Initially, it seemed as if all their efforts would backfire completely. Cassie became sullen and belligerent, continually threatening to run away or commit suicide, and she made no effort to find friends at her new school. After months of steady deterioration in their relationship, Cassie one day asked permission to go on a weekend religious retreat with her only friend at the new school. Reluctantly, her parents agreed.

To their astonishment, Cassie came back with an entirely new attitude, which she attributed to a conversion experience on the retreat. While there was still the occasional conflict over small matters, Cassie became cheerful and communicative at home, her grades improved at school, she forged new friendships and grew to be well liked and respected in her youth group, and she developed new interests in literature and photography. The change in her behavior was so dramatic that her parents agreed to her request to be transferred to public school at Columbine High School the next year. Although she was never preachy about her beliefs, Cassie had reasoned that she would have more opportunities to help others in public school because the students there were more in need of her Christian witness.

In the weeks after Harris and Klebold opened fire on their schoolmates at Columbine High in April of 1999—murdering Cassie along with twelve others and wounding twenty-three before taking their own lives—journalists and commentators around the nation indulged themselves in a prolonged frenzy of speculation about the underlying reasons for the rampage and what it told us about American society. A few representative newspaper headlines and editorials reflected this introspective mood: "Seeking the Answer to the Unanswerable"; "Are We at Fault As a Nation?"; "Kids Turn So Violent and High School Is So Hellish—Why?"[2] Popular candidates for the fundamental causes of the massacre included violence-drenched popular culture; lack of adequate gun-control regulations; and public school administrators too tolerant of a student culture of cliques and bullying.

It is not particularly surprising that a shocking incident like Columbine would be the occasion for an orgy of ruminations in the media about "root causes." Attributing such a tragedy to the aberrant behavior of a pair of defiant young men seems insufficient unto the phenomenon. And despite subsequent revisionist claims that the importance of Columbine was blown all out of proportion considering the slight statistical decrease in incidents of school violence in the past few years (after a big increase in recent decades), the general impression of its enormous significance was not in error, even if the explanations of what it signified were. It was clear to most Americans that the increasingly common nihilistic teen rage, for which Klebold and Harris became overnight symbols, represented the advent of something heretofore unknown in relatively affluent, peaceful communities like Littleton, Colorado.

What it represents is something that frightens many American parents, and not simply because this new level of suburban violence and nihilism makes them nervous when they send their children off to school every morning. As *Washington Post* columnist Donna Britt wrote not long after Columbine, "Much is made of how terrified parents are *for* their children. But few acknowledge how frightened we are *of* our children" (emphasis added). Britt was pondering the implications of a 1999 Kaiser Family Foundation survey of "Kids and the Media," which showed, among other disturbing findings, that 53 percent of children in the United States have televisions in their bedrooms (including 65 percent of eight- to eighteen-year-olds and 32 percent of kids between the ages of two and seven), and that the average child eight or older spends almost seven hours each day "being stroked, cajoled, and manipulated by TV, music, computers, video games, and reading materials" other than schoolwork.[3] For Britt, this constitutes clear evidence that many parents who are "balancing jobs, relationships, finances, and more" are turning to entertainment media to provide them with relief and to keep their children occupied. Judith Shulevitz of *Slate* magazine was more blunt: "Television is like air conditioning," she wrote. "You can't imagine how we ever survived without it. Chilled air made the South prosperous; television makes the dual-career or single-parent family possible."[4]

The problem, of course, is that unsupervised and often noxious electronic diversion is hardly an adequate substitute for parental care. In fact, the Kaiser study showed a strong correlation between heavy use of television and other media and "disputes with parents, unhappiness at school, and behavioral troubles" among children. Britt concludes that this finding, while not surprising, is at the root of both an increasing degree of alienation among children and a growing unease among parents:

> Less-contented kids may be more likely to take refuge in the media, to gorge themselves on make-believe worlds filled with

more danger and mayhem—and more wealth, fancy baubles,
and freedom without consequence—than their actual lives
could contain. Such images give kids more reason to fear and
to be dissatisfied with the real world when they finally flick
the "off" switch.[5]

Although Donna Britt was almost alone among American
journalists in suggesting so, it is true that most parents
regarded the Columbine horror as confirmation of their belief
that something had gone terribly wrong with the parent-
child relationship in the United States; that many parents
no longer knew their children very well; and that one of the
primary reasons for this estrangement was lack of parental
engagement in their lives. Despite the assurances of the media
and sociologists that children have not been negatively
affected by a vast shift of time and attention from home to
work in America over the past thirty years, most people worry
that professional obligations are preventing parents from
giving their children the attention they need; that children
are not faring well in our society; and that the decline in
their well-being is related to changes in the way they are
being brought up. In an NBC/*Wall Street Journal* poll taken
shortly after the Columbine massacre, a striking 83 percent
of Americans agreed that "parents not paying enough attention to what's going on in their children's lives" has become
"a very serious problem." The survey also showed that the
"breakdown of the family" ranked far above any other issue
as the biggest problem facing the country.[6] While parents
are increasingly relying on nonparental forms of child care,
evidently they are not very comfortable about doing so.

Former president Bill Clinton acknowledged the link
between Columbine and parental disengagement in a com-
mencement speech at Grambling State University. The ever
politically astute Clinton talked about "our around-the-world,
around-the-clock economy" in which "there just don't seem

to be enough hours in the day for parents to do everything they need to do." He spoke at length about one of the primary "challenges of the new economy"—the parental time deficit. "Because more and more parents are working outside the home," he noted, "they have less and less time for their children." Columbine must serve as a wake-up call, the president asserted, to remind Americans of the paramount importance of keeping the parent-child bond vital. "In the aftermath of the terrible tragedy at Littleton and the other school shootings we've had in our country," said Clinton, "they've forced us to confront the need not only to make guns less available to criminals and children, not only to make our culture less violent and our schools safer, but also to make the bonds that tie parents to children stronger."[7]

The specifics of the Columbine case affirmed the link between school violence and parental inattention. Dylan Klebold and Eric Harris came from relatively affluent homes in which both parents worked. The teenagers were allowed a great deal of autonomy. The Klebolds, who owned a home worth $500,000 and a fleet of seven cars—including four BMWs, one of them Dylan's own—had put their son in day care for several years before he started school. (When once asked to write a story related to childhood experiences in a Columbine High creative writing class, Dylan wrote a tale about Satan opening a day care center in hell.) The Harrises, for their part, left Eric undisturbed and unsupervised for long hours on the computer in his bedroom, designing his personal website and programming ever more complex and personalized versions of his favorite violent computer game, "Doom."

In the face of abundant warning signs, it seems that the Klebolds and the Harrises paid remarkably little attention to what their sons were up to in the months preceding their bloody attack. They were repeatedly made aware by school administrators, public authorities and other parents of the

boys' indulgence in violent, rage-filled, murderous fantasies
and other threatening behavior. The portents could hardly
have been clearer: the arrest of Dylan and Eric for breaking
into a van and stealing tools and electronic equipment; their
suspension from school for hacking into the school com-
puter system; their drinking and sneaking out at night; direc-
tions for the construction of bombs and obscenity-laden
threats of violence that Eric made against the school and
specific classmates on his personal website; the discovery of
a pipe bomb matching those website instructions behind
the Harris home; violent stories written for various classes
(including an essay that Dylan wrote describing an attack
on the school in terms remarkably similar to what was eventually carried out); a video made for a class project in which
Dylan and Eric dressed in trench coats, carried guns and pro-
ceeded to shoot fellow students in what turned out to be a
dry run for the real event.[8]

The parents were informed of all this aberrant activity, but
the two boys were still able to purchase numerous weapons
without detection and to wile away countless unsupervised
hours at the Harris home planning attacks on their classmates, watching violent movies, listening to music with lyrics
that glorify mass murder, and obsessively playing their own
customized version of "Doom."[9] They also managed to construct some ninety bombs without their parents' notice and
store them in their homes. Eric Harris's bedroom in particular was a veritable arsenal of poorly concealed weapons.[10]

Perhaps most astonishing of all is the videotape that Dylan
and Eric made in the weeks before their attack as a testament
to their rage. Drinking from a bottle of Jack Daniels and sitting
side by side in basement recliners after their parents had gone
to bed, they gave vent to their many hatreds and their desire
for fame. They also anticipated what their attack would be like
and the effects it would have on their families, their friends
and society at large. While their contempt for humanity

in general and their classmates in particular comes across as chillingly impersonal—a posture learned from the world of violent entertainment in which they had immersed them- selves—it is their attitude toward their parents that is most telling. As they went further and further toward translating their fantasies of bloody retribution into hideous reality— making detailed plans and accumulating weapons and ammu- nition—their parents were so easily fooled as to win only pity and contempt.

"Thank God my parents never searched my room," Harris says on the video. The boys recount the ease with which they built their arsenal. Klebold recalls the time he was interrupted while modeling his black leather trench coat with his sawed- off shotgun barely concealed: "They didn't even know it was there." Harris relates how his mother once saw him carrying a gym bag with a gun handle sticking out—and assumed it was his BB gun. There was also the time that an employee of Green Mountain Guns called the Harris home and Eric's father answered the phone. According to Eric, when the clerk informed his father that "his clips were in," Mr. Harris sim- ply told the clerk that he hadn't ordered any clips, without bothering to ask whether he had the right number. If his father had asked just one question, "we would've been f—ed," says Eric. "We wouldn't be able to do what we're going to do," Kle- bold agrees. The boys display a casual confidence that they can get away with whatever they want. "People have no clue," Klebold says incredulously on one tape. "I could convince them that I'm going to climb Mount Everest, or I have a twin brother growing out of my back," adds Harris.

Klebold predicts that his parents will one day watch the tape they are making and wish they had intervened: "If only we could have reached them sooner or found this tape," he imag- ines them saying. "If only we would have searched their room," adds Harris. "If only we would have asked the right questions." But the boys insist that their parents are powerless to prevent what they are about to do. "There's nothing you guys could've done to prevent this," Harris says, contradicting what he has already related about their inattentiveness. Then he declares, "My parents are the best f—ing parents I have ever known. My dad is great. I wish I was a f—ing sociopath so I didn't have any remorse, but I do.... This is going to tear them apart.... I really am sorry about all this.... It f—ing sucks to do this to them." Harris clearly understands that it is his parents, not he himself, who will bear the consequences of his suicidal final act. "They're going to go through hell once we're finished. They're never going to see the end of it."

Klebold expresses the same sentiments, promising his parents that there is nothing they could have done to stop what would happen: "You can't understand what we feel; you can't understand no matter how much you think you can. It's my life. They gave it to me, I can do with it what I want.... If they don't like it, I'm sorry, but that's too bad." Despite their lack of comprehension about his life, Klebold credits his parents with giving him the sense of autonomy he so values. His mom and dad have been "great parents" who taught him "self-awareness, self-reliance.... I always appreciated that." But it seems that this lesson in independence, which in Klebold's case started quite early, came at a high price. "I'm sorry I have so much rage," he tells them. "If you could see all the anger I've stored over the past four f—ing years." Anger that had its roots further back than they might imagine—as far back as the Foothills Day Care Center, filled with the "stuck-up" kids he felt hated him. "Being shy didn't help.... I'm going to kill you all. You've been giving us s— for years."

Despite the clues that this tape provided, the many commentators who speculated liberally about "the causes of Columbine" scarcely mentioned the possibility that inattentive or absentee parenting was in any way to blame. Most of those who brought it up at all did so only to deny explicitly that it was relevant to this case. Columnist Ellen Goodman, for instance, sneered at the idea that the parents were in any way responsible for what happened, although she acknowledged that "advocates of parental responsibility laws seem to have found their poster parents." Arguing that parents can err just as seriously by being too controlling or intrusive as by being negligent, Goodman asserted that "the Klebolds and the Harrises were not Fagin-like adults who set up their sons in the business of murder. We hold them responsible rather for what they did not know and did not do." She went on to quote a Little League coach to the effect that "Eric's parents are what we could call dream parents" and a pastor who portrayed the Klebolds as "hard-working, very intelligent."[11]

This was, in fact, the theme of much of the coverage relating to the "lessons" of Columbine: that the Klebolds and Harrises, by all accounts, were excellent parents, and that to spotlight inattentive parenting as an explanation of their sons' crimes was to ignore the truth that such a tragedy could befall *any* family. A typical example was the in-depth *Washington Post* article published barely a week after the boys stormed the school. According to the author, neighbors of both Klebold and Harris seemed to believe that if this could happen to these families, it could happen to anyone. "We are all one bullet and one pipe bomb away from the agony of Wayne and Kathy Harris," a former neighbor said, adding that the Harrises were "great neighbors ... always raking their leaves, shoveling their sidewalk, lending a hand in a pinch." The Klebolds, it was noted, refused to let their two boys play with guns. Another neighbor said of them: "Wonderful family. All the positives you can imagine."[12] One report quoted an investigator as saying, "They were not absentee parents. They're normal people who seem to care for their children and were involved in their life." In numerous other articles, child development experts were trotted out to make the case that the jock-centered culture of Columbine High,

where status was conferred according to athletic achievement, and a lack of adequate counseling services in the school
were far more likely culprits than parental negligence.

Given the united front on the part of the media, the question arises: why such a need to minimize the role played in
this tragedy by indifferent parenting? Why the strange impulse
to deny a phenomenon that most Americans regard as so central to the problems of youth and families in our culture?

I would contend that this denial has everything to do with
a longstanding investment by a significant number of influential people—represented disproportionately in the opin-
ion-making classes of the media, academia and the social
sciences—in what amounts to a vast and unprecedented
social experiment. It is an experiment that has pursued an
ideal of absolute equality of economic opportunity and
advancement for males and females, based on the assump-
tion that women are no different from men in the realm of
family responsibilities or childrearing ability or obligations.
It has proposed dual-income families as a social norm—a
vision of society in which every adult pursues his or her opti-
mum career advancement, earnings potential and personal
fulfillment in the market economy outside the home—with
the necessary result that even very young children are left
for a large part of the day without parental care and attention. This experiment is sometimes spoken about elliptically
in terms of its impact on parents: the draining physical and
emotional effects of such a regimen; the difficulty that adults
experience in achieving a proper "work/family balance" in
our economy; the need to expand after-school programs for
children because of parents' busy work schedules; or the
"child care crisis," that is, the supposed lack of affordable,
high-quality child care for the children of working parents.
It is seldom discussed in terms of its effects on children. Ironically—and perversely—in his musings about Satan open-

ing a day care center in hell, Dylan Klebold showed a keener awareness of the consequences of absentee parenting for children and society than most commentaries you are likely to read about the "child care crisis."

"OF ALL THE EXPLOSIVE SUBJECTS in America today," social critic Mary Eberstadt has written, "none is as cordoned off, as surrounded by rhetorical landmines, as the question of whether and just how much children need their parents—especially their mothers." What George Will has termed a "lethal reticence" continues to smother discussions of this topic. While it's common to hear about the insidious influence of the media, of "youth culture," of exclusive peer groups, of school environment and teacher incompetence, and even (more commonly in recent years) of broken family backgrounds, it is rare indeed to hear any suggestion that lack of parental engagement with and devotion to young children is in any way to blame for the increasing dysfunctional behavior among adolescents.

The connection, however, is clear for all those who care to see it. As Eberstadt says, "Over the past few decades, more and more parents have been spending less and less time at home, and most measures of what social scientists call 'child well-being' have simultaneously been in what once would have been judged scandalous decline."[13] Indeed, it would be hard to contest the assertion that life as a child today in "the country with the highest standard of living the world has ever known" has become a remarkably dangerous proposition. As child education expert William Damon notes, "the litany is now so well-known that it is losing its power to shock."[14] The United States has the highest rate of both child homicide and child suicide in the industrialized world. The childhood murder rate has tripled since 1950.[15] Children "born and raised in the 1970s were three to four times more likely to commit suicide as people that age had been at mid-century," estimates Harvard sociologist Robert Putnam.[16]

A 1995 study of adolescent sexual activity showing that a young person's first sexual experimentation most often occurs at home in the parents' absence concludes: "It appears that an empty and unsupervised home provides more opportunity for the adolescent as well as for the younger grade-school latch-key child to engage in sex."[17] The number of sexually active teenagers has also risen substantially: in 1955, one-quarter of girls eighteen and under were sexually experienced; today, the number reporting that they have had sexual intercourse is 50 percent for girls, 55 percent for boys.[18]

Kay Hymowitz points to a link between absentee parents and sexual activity among adolescents by referring to an outbreak of syphilis among a group of two hundred sexually active teens in prosperous Rockdale County, Georgia. She notes that most of their parents "were out of the house working long hours to provide their children with lavish homes, cars, cell phones, and the latest teen fashions. Most of the sex parties took place after school between 3:00 P.M. and 7:00 P.M., in houses emptied of working adults. Other times, kids slipped out of the house after midnight, without waking their exhausted parents."[19]

Other research has shown that parents' absence from the house when children come home from school substantially increases the risk of substance abuse, violence and suicide. The Census Bureau says that seven million children between the ages of five and fourteen routinely care for themselves at home after school before their parents return from work.[20] In a 1994 volume of *Pediatric Annals*, physicians Elizabeth M. Aldeman and Stanford B. Friedman of Albert Einstein College of Medicine studied the surprisingly high incidence of sexual experimentation, drug use and delinquency in teens from affluent families and concluded that "being home alone without supervision may predispose [adolescents] to these behaviors" because "their parents may be preoccupied socially or professionally, and may not make the necessary quality time for them at home."[21] Sociologist Mark Warr of the University of Texas confirmed this finding in another study that sought to correlate the time parents spend with children and the rate of juvenile delinquency. He concluded that "contemporary arguments notwithstanding, small amounts of quality time may not be sufficient to offset the criminogenic aspects of peer culture to which adolescents are commonly exposed."[22]

There are also signs of a link between the increase in mental health problems among children and a decline in time spent with parents. A January 2001 report from the surgeon general referred to a "public crisis in mental care for children and adolescents," citing a marked increase in diagnosed illnesses, especially "conduct disorders," believed to affect millions of teenage and preteen boys.[23] Some recent studies have attributed various mental illnesses in children—ranging from depression to "borderline psychopathology"—to lack of parental attention.[24] The Children's Defense Fund estimated in 1995 that 7.7 million American children suffer from emotional disorders.[25]

In addition to the rise in behavioral and emotional problems, the rates of sexual abuse of children have also gone up sharply, some estimates showing a 350 percent increase since 1980.[26] Once again, the link to parental absence is clear. After noting the studies showing that children are much likelier to be victims of sexual abuse from cohabiting males who are not biologically related, Mary Eberstadt points out that "in order for predatory males (and they are almost always males) to abuse, they must first have access; and that the increasing absence from the home of biological mothers—who statistically speaking almost never violate children in this way—effectively increases the access of would-be predators."[27]

A handful of other scholars and writers have tentatively drawn the connection between increased parental absence and a historically unprecedented decline in child well-being. Harvard's Robert Putnam attributes the phenomenal rate of child suicide to "social isolation," pointing to a study sponsored by the Sloan Foundation showing that the average American teenager is alone about three and a half hours every day, which means that "adolescents spend more time alone than with family and friends."[28] By one estimate, the number of "latch-key" children, unattended at home for much of the day after school, rose from 1.6 million in 1976 to 12 million in 1994.[29] Francis Fukuyama makes the link explicit in his recent book *The Great Disruption:* "There have been losses accompanying the gains [of mothers leaving the house for the workplace], and those losses have fallen disproportionately on children."[30] Child development authority Dr. T. Berry Brazelton asserts that "never before has one generation been less healthy, less cared for, less prepared for life than their parents were at the same age."[31]

But these warnings were drowned out by agenda-driven social science. As married women with children entered the workforce in ever-higher numbers and the time children spent in nonmaternal care increased, the argument about the importance of "quality time" began to be heard. Feminist advocates of the working-mother model of social organization claimed that quantity of time spent with a child was irrelevant to that child's well-being; what mattered was that the *quality* of such time be pleasant, mutually enriching and formative. It was fine if the modern career mom didn't spend as much time with the kids as the dominating, overprotective housewife-mom of the 1950s, perhaps even better, as long as the time together was "quality time."

The fallacy of this argument was obvious from the start. As child development expert Dr. Penelope Leach says, "The younger the child, the more impossible it is to schedule togetherness time. You cannot make a tired baby stay awake for a day's worth of cuddling, and trying may be a selfish attempt to salve adult consciences and conflicts at the expense of overstimulated infants." In addition, infants and toddlers can't conform their needs to the parent's availability: "You cannot easily persuade a one year old who wanted you to play with him this morning to take his one and only chance to play right now; if he is angry at your desertion, he will not let you off the hook that easily."[32] Aside from the fact that young children have constant needs for care and attention that cannot be scheduled into quality blocks, the whole notion of "quality time" assumes that parental influence on a child's development can be telescoped into a series of intense moments without losing its formative impact. Most parents are keenly aware, however, that the less time they spend with their children, the greater the role of secondary influences on the children's beliefs and behavior.

Surveys of working parents show that they have never been completely sold on the idea that pursuing their dual careers does not exact a price from their children. Half of all parents, according to a 1995 Gallup poll, feel that they do not spend enough time with their children; for employed parents, the proportion is two-thirds. The same survey showed that only one-third of the respondents ate dinner with their children on a regular basis.[33] An extensive *Los Angeles Times* survey of parents in 1999 found that "having enough time to spend with children" ranked as the top "important problem facing parents raising children today," above even "making sure children get good education."[34] A Families and Work Institute survey from 1993 showed that among those parents working more than forty hours a week, 74 percent said they lacked "enough time with children."[35]

Parents' anxiety is shared by the children themselves. A recent study published in the *Journal of the American Medical Association* concluded that teens who feel their parents pay attention to them are less likely to use drugs, drink alcohol, smoke or have sex.[36] Another study showed that although half of the nation's youth watch television more than two hours a day, three-fourths of these children say that they would choose more time with their parents if they had the option.[37] And a recent survey of sixth- through twelfth-graders showed that 20 percent of them had not had a conversation longer than ten minutes with either of their parents in more than a month.[38]

As evidence accumulated that parental absence was indeed related to declining child welfare, the "quality time" argument has become increasingly untenable. Consequently, advocates of the career-mom model subtly changed the terms of the debate. Ellen Galinsky, a longtime advocate of career mothers and commercial day care, argues in *Ask the Children: What America's Children Really Think about Working Parents* (1999) that children are relatively unconcerned about a lack of time with their working parents, and that the perception of parents to the contrary is based on unwarranted guilt. Galinsky uses over a thousand interviews with children between the ages of eight and eighteen to contend that kids are more worried about the job-related stress their working parents bring home than they are about the shrinking amount of time those parents devote to them. After having, in effect, asked these children how they should best be raised, Galinsky draws the conclusion that the old debate over quality versus quantity of time—a debate originated by feminist advocates of child care and working mothers like Galinsky herself—should be discarded as antiquated. But despite the change in emphasis, the gist of the argument remained the same: that the amount of time parents devote to their children does not determine their welfare, and that complete devotion to career is perfectly compatible with fully attentive parenthood, if only the right public policies are implemented.[39]

This rhetorical shift—an attempt to counter the accumulating evidence that parental absence does indeed have adverse effects on children—coincided with a concerted effort by feminist scholars to argue that, despite all proof to the contrary, parental absence has really not increased at all since the advent of the duel-career family in the United States. This effort took aim at data collected by sociologist John Robinson of the University of Maryland that showed a drop in the hours that parents spent with their children from 30 hours to just 17 hours per week between 1965 and 1985.[40] The data reported by Robinson track very closely to an earlier study by Victor Fuchs at Stanford showing a loss of 10 to 12 hours per week in parental time with children between 1960 and 1986, which Fuchs said was largely attributable to the entry of more mothers into the workplace. The trend toward less parental time for children was confirmed by a 1999 report to the president from the Council of Economic Advisors finding that American parents on average had 22 fewer hours per week to spend at home compared with thirty years earlier, largely as a result of a sharp upturn in married mothers' participation in the paid labor force.[41]

A widely reported study from the University of Michigan in 2000 claimed to debunk the "myth" of declining parental time with children. When these findings were released to the press, chief researcher Sandra Hofferth made the purpose of the study explicit: to prove that parents pursuing the dual-career or the single-parent family model do just as well when it comes to fulfilling their responsibilities as do parents in more traditional households. "A lot of people out there say that because of changes in families, mothers and fathers are spending less time with children," she was quoted in one newspaper story. "There was no actual evidence for it."[42] Her study purported to show not only an overall increase in time spent with children by both working and nonworking mothers since 1981, but also that children with two working parents spend only three hours less time a week with mom and dad than children with a stay-at-home parent.

Most time-strapped parents would disagree. In the first place, they would find the way that "time with children" was measured highly suspect. In response to one query about her methodology, Hofferth specified that "the time that was quoted is just the time directly engaged with children—caring for, reading to, taking along on errands. It does not count the time you are with your child but not directly doing something with him—such as preparing meals while the child is watching television."[43] In other words, parental *presence* (doing chores in another room) does not count as being "engaged." Since the study "focuses on an individual child's time with the mother, the father, or either parent, but not on total time with children," it grossly distorts the actual "social ecology" of childrearing. Essentially, this odd way of measuring time spent with children implies that there is no difference between a 1960s mother being available to her three children for nine hours a day and a 1990s mother being available to her one child for three hours a day.

The University of Michigan study also puts all employed mothers into a single category rather than stipulating differences between those employed part-time and those employed full-time. Since the time that mothers employed part-time spend with their children is much closer to that of stay-at-home mothers, conflating all "working moms" into a single category masks the comparatively low amount of time that mothers employed full-time spend with their children.

Interestingly, the study actually does acknowledge that the effect of full-time maternal employment in reducing children's time with their mothers is "quite large," a finding that received little notice amid all the attention given to the other finding of a purported "increase" in parental time. The fact is that Hofferth and others tend to paint a rosy picture of how time-strapped working mothers cope with their childrearing responsibilities by de-emphasizing the large and growing disparities between "highly involved" parents (generally, homemakers, moms employed part-time and married fathers) and "often-absent" parents (generally, mothers employed full-time, single parents and—especially—noncustodial parents).

MARY EBERSTADT RECENTLY POINTED OUT that "forty years ago, most Americans would surely have never believed that in the not-so-distant future, the majority of mothers with babies and preschool children would end up parting company with those children for many or most of their waking hours, and that many of these same mothers would also insist that the separation itself was positively good for their child." Eberstadt argues that this "maternal absenteeism" is historically unprecedented, an unnatural condition that is "conscious, counterintuitive, learned." In her view, this "mother-child separation" is probably "the most important domestic experiment of our time."[44] Dr. Stanley Greenspan puts it in equally unequivocal terms: "Our society has launched into a monumental experiment that has the potential to change who we are and how we function as individuals and therefore how our communities and, indeed, how our society will work in the future."[45]

As Eberstadt indicates, the clearest sign of the revolutionary new attitude toward the upbringing of children is the increasing reliance on nonparental, institutional care for infants and toddlers. When political figures such as former First Lady Hillary Clinton talk about the problem of parental absence, they have in mind the "child care crisis" that they believe can be alleviated by heavier public investment in day care. But in fact, the sharp increase in the use of day care over the last three decades corresponds to the increase in child pathologies over that period. If parental absence and declining interaction with children are closely related to our crisis in child well-being, it only stands to reason that the increasing reliance on institutional day care as a stand-in for parents is part and parcel of the problem.

Ironically, even many advocates of government-supported institutional day care for preschoolers agree with this proposition. Dr. Edward Zigler, director of the Bush Center for Child Development and Social Policy at Yale University, asserts that the years children spend in low-quality day care is a major cause of the biggest increase in the rate of child violence and depression that our country has ever witnessed.[46] Zigler's opinion counts. He was a cofounder of Head Start, the preschool program designed to give children from under-privileged backgrounds an intellectual and developmental boost in their preparation for school. In a very real sense (which we will examine in more depth in the chapters that follow), the true debate over institutional day care is whether the unarguably sub-par system that exists can be improved with more subsidies, or whether it is inherently flawed and detrimental to children.

How widespread is out-of-home care? Today, over twelve million preschoolers are in some regular child care arrangement other than maternal care at home. That figure constitutes 63 percent of the entire preschool population of the United States.[47] According to one recent survey, more than half of this child care population spends 35 hours or more per week in nonmaternal day care arrangements, and over a third are placed in two or more nonparental day care arrangements each week.[48] Seven out of ten of the nonmaternal care arrangements entail someone other than the father providing care; over half of them entail care by someone other than a relative. And the nonrelative care of preschoolers is becoming more and more industrialized. In 1995, for the first time on record, the percentage of preschool children cared for in organized facilities was higher than the percentage in less formal nonrelative care, such as family-run day care or nannies in or out of the child's home, and it remains significantly higher. The proportion of parents using day care for their children has tripled since 1970.[49] As recently as the mid-1960s, care of infants and toddlers outside of the home was so unusual that most states refused even to license facilities for children under three years of age.[50] Today, well over half of this same group receives care outside the parents' home and a majority of three- to five-year-olds receive some care in a center-based program.[51] In addition, the percentage of infants and toddlers in day care is going up faster than any other group.

Day care is a booming business in the United States, with over five hundred thousand establishments taking in over $13 billion a year and serving almost seven million children.[52] According to the Census Bureau, during the parents' work day, the average time per week that children under five spend in the care of family members is 23 hours; the average time they spend in nonrelative care is 39 hours—almost the equivalent of a full work week.[53] Of all the different types of arrangements, preschoolers with working moms spent the most time in day care centers (35 hours per week).[54]

Advocates of commercial day care often assert that the relevant consideration is not the amount of time that children spend in day care, but rather the *quality* of the care they receive there. Hence the push for improving the day care system with an infusion of government support. But this argument is much like the claim that "quality time" with parents is more important to children than quantity, and it is equally dubious. New research confirms the long-held correlation between hours spent in preschool day care (whatever the "quality") and increased problem behavior and physiological signs of stress in young children.[55]

According to numerous published studies, only 10 to 15 percent of available day care is of even adequate quality; the percentage of good-quality day care available for infants and toddlers is even lower. A study from the University of Colorado summarizes the grave consequences of poor-quality care for children younger than four years of age: "Babies in poor-quality rooms are vulnerable to more illness because basic sanitary conditions are not met for diapering and feeding; are endangered because of safety problems that exist in the room; miss warm, supportive relationships with adults; and lose out on learning because they lack the books and toys required for physical and intellectual growth."[56] This is a vital point, since child development experts across the spectrum, whatever their position on outside-the-home care, agree that the first three years are a crucially formative period, and that inadequate care during this time has lasting detrimental effects on emotional, intellectual and physical development.

Child development expert Stanley Greenspan sums up the developmental needs of babies and young children in six major areas:

1. Sights, sounds, touches, and other sensations tailored to the baby's unique nervous system in order to foster attention, awareness, learning, language, and self-control.
2. An ongoing, loving, intimate relationship (lasting years, not months) with one or a few caregivers in order to develop caring, empathy, and trust.
3. Interactions with adults made up of long sequences of back-and-forth smiles, voice tone, gestures, sounds, reaching, and the like. These "emotional dialogues" foster the beginnings of purposefulness, a sense of self, and logical communications.
4. Long negotiations with gestures and eventually gestures and words to solve problems, which foster early types of thinking and social skills.
5. Pretend play and spontaneous exchanges of ideas between a caregiver and a child in order to foster language and creativity.

6. Logical use of ideas through a caregiver's eliciting a child's opinion and debates in order to promote logical thinking, planning, and readiness for math and reading.[57]

Greenspan concludes that meeting these essential needs depends upon a kind of emotional interaction that is all but impossible to achieve in a day care setting, but is "almost automatic" in families. In large part, this is because the high turnover rate of day care workers and the high ratio of children per worker in commercial child care do not allow for the type of attachment to a primary caregiver that experts agree is vital for the normal development of children three and under. (In day care centers considered to have an excellent child-to-staff ratio, a typical caregiver will have responsibility for four or more toddlers.) Yet it is precisely for children in this age group that the use of day care has expanded most rapidly in recent years. A study from 1995 showed that 44 percent of infants under one year old are now in nonparental care for an average of 31 hours a week. Among four- to five-year-olds, 84 percent were in nonparental care for an average of 28 hours.[58]

What one analyst has called "caregiver roulette" is endemic in commercial day care, an inherent aspect of the economy of scale that allows the system to function at all. A recent government-funded study noted that "infants in care typically experienced more than two nonparental arrangements during the first year of life" and that "over one-third of the infants who began nonparental care before their first birthday experienced three or more different arrangements with providers other than parents." These frequent changes in child care arrangements are cause for "concern," since previous research has established that "children with more childcare changes are more frequently classified as insecurely attached, are less competent than peers as toddlers, are more withdrawn and aggressive in preschool, and have more problems in school as first graders" than children with more stable care arrangements.[59] The same report judges that "the highest level of positive caregiving was provided by in-home caregivers, including fathers and grandparents caring for only one child, closely followed by home-based arrangements with relatively few children per adult"—that is, the forms of care that are becoming less and less common, while use of commercial day care continues to expand.

We are just beginning to see the consequences of this enormous, unprecedented shift toward a new and basically untested way of rearing and socializing very young children. Yet there is nothing approaching a vigorous debate about the explosive growth of day care in the media, in academia or in the political world.

Former CBS news correspondent Bernard Goldberg has called the decline of parental influence over children "the most important story you never saw on TV." He concludes that the major media find any open questioning of the assumptions behind our experiment in the nonparental rearing of children to be culturally—and commercially—unacceptable. But Goldberg sees something else at work besides fear of offending the public:

> It is that the media elites will not take on feminists. Feminists are the pressure group that the media elites (and their wives and friends) are most aligned with.... America's newsrooms are filled with women who drop their kids off someplace before they go to work or leave them at home with the nanny. These journalists are not just defending working mothers—*they're defending themselves!*[60]

The same could be said of sociological researchers who have proven so influential in other debates on family issues. Their approach to the day care question has been much like their treatment of the single-mother issue. For many years, the academic left insisted that single motherhood had no detrimental effects on children, and that the problems associated with illegitimacy were entirely due to social stigma and the resulting economic and racial discrimination. When the Moynihan Report in 1965 famously warned that illegitimacy—especially fatherless adolescent males—was the primary threat to the further advancement of the African-American community, the sociology faculties in universities across the country were outraged. They claimed that the "matriarchal family" was simply an adaptation of the white "nuclear family" to black social circumstances and mores. Yet at the same time, they demanded more funding of programs designed to support those same asymmetrical families, such as Head Start, day care and after-school programs.

Today we see in academia the same kind of intellectual inconsistencies and intolerance of dissent in the debate—or lack of it—over institutional day care. A sweeping social experiment with profound consequences for young children and their families has been pushed beyond the reach of open and honest discussion.

TWO

An Intolerable Truth

t is a truism among politicians and pundits that reform of the Social Security system is the "third rail" of American politics: touch it and you die. In academic circles, the same principle applies to evidence that day care has detrimental effects on children. It's understood that you simply "don't go there" if you know what's good for you.

Jay Belsky, one of the chief researchers for the recent child care study sponsored by the National Institute of Child Health and Human Development, found this out first-hand. Now a sociology professor at the University of London and one of the world's foremost experts on child development, Belsky is a veteran of the day care controversy. When just starting his career as a researcher in the late 1970s and early 1980s, he won praise for work that seemed to show that children suffered no measurable detrimental effects from organized day care. Belsky began to be regarded as a day care champion, and advocates frequently cited his research to argue that care outside the home was perfectly all right for children. He was even given a prestigious award by colleagues in the American Psychological Association.

A few years later, this rising star in the field of child development research at Pennsylvania State University began to suspect that the story wasn't that simple. What he termed "a slow, steady trickle of evidence" had begun to convince him that long hours in day care, particularly for very young

42

children, could be a risk factor for behavioral problems later on. As each isolated negative indication came in, he was able to discover methodological reasons to dismiss the findings. But "it got to the point," he later said, "where I felt like a pretzel, twisting and turning, trying to explain these things away. By 1986, I said, 'I can't do this anymore.'"[1]

Belsky published his tentative conclusions—calling for more research on the matter—in a relatively obscure newsletter under the headline "Infant Day Care: A Cause for Concern?" He was wholly unprepared for the firestorm that followed. His peers accused him of being a hardline opponent of day care, an enemy of women working and a closet misogynist. As a result of the episode, Belsky's reputation dipped and he found himself shunned at scientific meetings. Overnight, he became *persona non grata*.

Although Belsky subsequently published various studies and findings that were, quite obviously, not the product of an ideologue with an axe to grind against day care, the reputation stuck. In the intensely politicized world of child care research, it was enough that he had even raised the question of whether detrimental effects were possible. To many of his fellow sociologists, he stood convicted as an adversary of working mothers. Belsky objected to this characterization of his work, pointing out that he was simply going where the findings took him, just as any objective researcher should. But many of his colleagues marked him down as one who couldn't be trusted to stick to what Kay Hymowitz calls the "new life script for American women," one which entails uninterrupted careers for mothers while their young children thrive in "quality" day care.[2]

Belsky had always been enormously uncomfortable with attempts by both sides in the public debate over child care policy to use sociological research to make their case, arguing that researchers have to be very careful about lending themselves and their work to groups with political agendas.[3]

In fact, this was happening all too frequently among his staunchly feminist colleagues in the sociology departments of American universities and in editorial positions at academic journals, as Belsky himself could now testify.

In 1999, to take just one example, a study was published in the prestigious American Psychological Association journal *Developmental Psychology* analyzing the effects of maternal employment on child development.[4] Immediately upon its publication, all the major news media reported its findings: that absolutely no detrimental effects on children resulted from their mothers' employment outside the home. Typical of the coverage was a story on *CBS Evening News* that began, "A new study shows children of women who work outside the home do just as well as those with stay-at-home moms."[5] Headlines in newspapers across the country echoed that assessment. The *Washington Post* proclaimed, "Mothers' Employment Works for Children: Study Finds No Long-Term Damage."[6] The *Atlanta Journal and Constitution* bannered, "Working Moms Not Shortchanging Kids, Study Suggests."[7] The *Star-Ledger* in Newark, New Jersey, confidently proclaimed, "Keep Your Day Job, Mom: Study Suggests Kids Will Be Fine."[8] Those who didn't know better would have been forced to conclude that this "comprehensive" and "multiyear" effort had definitively vindicated day care.

The study's author, Elizabeth Harvey, then an assistant professor of psychology at the University of Massachusetts at Amherst, confirmed this impression in interviews with over fifty major news outlets, including CBS, NBC, CNN and the BBC. "Working mothers have a lot of guilt," she told the *Boston Globe,* adding that she hoped the study would "alleviate some of that guilt."[9] In another interview, Harvey emphasized that her study had given day care a clean bill of health. "I found there was no difference between children whose mothers were employed versus children whose mothers were not employed during the first three years," she told the Associated Press. "Being employed is not going to harm the children in any way."[10]

In fact, her study showed nothing of the sort. The data that Harvey relied on had been gleaned from the ongoing National Longitudinal Surveys first commissioned to study the workforce in the 1960s; no separate study had been conducted relating specifically to day care. Compared with the general population, the mothers used in her sample were twice as likely to be black or Hispanic and twice as likely to be single mothers. Their family income was less than half the national norm. They were significantly younger and well below average in intelligence.[11] Moreover, the emotional assessment of the children in these families was based primarily on what their mothers told government interviewers.

As several commentators later noted, the children in the sample may already have been "at risk" for performing poorly on cognitive and behavioral tests because of emotional, social and economic deprivation. If anything, they pointed out, a finding of "no difference" between the children of mothers who work and those of mothers who stay at home might indicate that some of the negative effects of maternal employment on children are muted in a family context that is already less than optimal. Also, David Murray of the Statistical Assessment Service reported that Harvey, by lumping together mothers who worked only a few hours each week with those who worked up to forty hours, had "lowered the bar" for what differences in test results among the children counted as "statistically significant."[12] "If you set out to find nothing," Murray observed, "this is a good way to do it."[13]

Harvey herself later acknowledged that some of the concerns about her study were legitimate, but maintained that she had clearly pointed out the sample's limitations in her article and warned against generalizing from her conclusions.[14] Pregnant at the time and planning to put her own child in day care, she justified her unqualified remarks in interviews by saying that the nuances of her study were too "complex" for reporters to understand. Those complex nuances, however, did not deter the American Psychological Association, which originally ran Harvey's study in its flagship journal, from giving it a ringing endorsement. The APA press release on the study opened with the equally unqualified statement: "A mother's employment outside the home has no significant negative effect on her children."[15]

At the very time it accepted Harvey's submission, the APA journal, *Developmental Psychology,* turned down another study dealing with some of the negative effects of nonmaternal care, this one authored by Jay Belsky. The source for Belsky's data was the continuing government-funded study of children in day care, conducted by academic researchers nationwide in coordination with the National Institute of Child Health and Human Development (NICHD). Ironically, Carolyn Zahn-Waxler, then editor of *Developmental Psychology,* rejected Belsky's article because of a "lack of assessment of type and quality of child care"—distinctions completely accounted for in Belsky's NICHD data but omitted in Harvey's study. While Harvey's work was trumpeted in major media reports across the nation, Belsky's study, eventually published in the well-respected journal *Psychology,* got virtually no mention in the press. As Belsky said at the time, "There's gatekeeping going on. The intelligentsia has decided that we don't want mothers to feel bad about their decisions. So let's give them the good news over and over again." He concluded that his colleagues in the research community were, in essence, carefully managing the coverage of the issue with willing cooperation from a day care–friendly media: "If [Harvey's] study had shown the opposite—that children are harmed by day care—rest assured, it would have been dismissed with such dispatch that the media wouldn't have covered it at all."[16]

JAY BELSKY'S DISGUST AT THE apparent bias against approaches and conclusions deemed politically incorrect may very well have contributed to his decision to leave Pennsylvania State University for the University of London in 2000, to take a position as the founding director of the Institute for the Study of Children, Families and Social Issues at Birkbeck College. But if he hoped to avoid becoming embroiled in more controversy with his move to England, he was disabused of that notion in fairly short order when some of the results of the ongoing study conducted by the National Institute of Child Health and Human Development were made public in the spring of 2001.

The government-sponsored study has been advertised as the largest and most comprehensive ever conducted of early child care and child development. Beginning in 1991, twenty-five researchers at ten U.S. universities—collectively known as the NICHD Early Child Care Research Network—have tracked 1,364 children, following both their development and their care arrangements from infancy. Although most of the subjects of the study would enter sixth grade in the fall of 2002, data were analyzed only through the children's first five years. The early findings of the ongoing project, which has cost taxpayers $80 million thus far, have already yielded dozens of academic papers by the researchers connected with the study on subjects such as the relation of child care arrangements to maternal attachment and child behavior.

Some of the preliminary reports from the NICHD study were accepted for presentation at the annual meeting of the Society for Research in Child Development, in April of 2001 in Minneapolis. The director of policy and communication for the meeting, Lauren Fasig, set up a press conference on April 18 for reporters interested in the latest findings, only to find that most of the researchers, still in transit to the

meeting, were unavailable. But Fasig was able to secure the
services of two of the principal researchers who were already
in town: Dr. Sarah Friedman, scientific coordinator for the
entire project, and Belsky, who had been one of the primary
researchers from the project's inception. It was decided that
Belsky would present the findings related to quantity of nonmaternal child care, while Friedman would address the effects
of quality differences in care.

Belsky's fortuitous availability resulted in perhaps the first
public glimpse into the ideological intolerance and institutional corruption that pervade the strange world of child
care research. At the Minneapolis press conference, Friedman reported that the study found that children in high-
quality care received a cognitive advantage in language and
memory skills over those not in high-quality care (but not,
as news stories later maintained, over those in parental care)—
a finding that might seem self-evident. Friedman's emphasis on this finding was in keeping with the tone of previous
NICHD reports touting the advantages of high-quality day
care, along with recommendations of greater government
investment to make that high-quality care more available.

What followed, however, went astray from the official
script. In his presentation, Belsky pointed out the strong correlation between longer hours in nonmaternal care and
behavioral problems—specifically, "aggressive" and "noncompliant" behavior such as "talks too much," "argues a
lot," "temper tantrums," "demands a lot of attention," "dis-
rupts class discipline," "cruelty," "meanness," "bullying,"
"explosive behavior" and "gets in lots of fights." Specifically,
researchers found that children in day care for extended periods (defined as more than 30 hours per week) were almost
three times as likely to exhibit these behavioral problems as
children with minimal time in nonmaternal care (less than
10 hours per week). Belsky noted that this increased risk of
problem behavior could not be attributed to maternal

depression, poverty or the poor quality of day care, all of which had been controlled for in the study. This was highly significant because all these factors had been used to explain away disparities in previous research. "There is a constant dose-response relationship between time in care and problem behavior," Belsky explained, "especially those involving aggressive behavior."

In fact, studies over the previous twenty years had pointed to similar negative effects of mother-absence on child development, but much of this information had been buried in obscure academic journals. Media coverage of earlier research on the topic, aided and abetted by researchers themselves, had always stressed a supposed lack of any basis for believing that spending long hours away from their mothers daily is in any way harmful to children. So the new findings that Belsky was announcing—the first time a large, highly publicized, government-sponsored study had pointed to anything negative about nonmaternal care—were bound to make some waves.

They did. The clinching moment came when Belsky was asked by a reporter about the implications of the findings. "If more time in all sorts of [child-care] arrangements is predicting disconcerting outcomes," he responded, "then if you want to reduce the probability of those outcomes, you reduce the time in care. Extend parental leave and part time work."

According to observers, a look of abject horror passed over Sarah Friedman's face. "On behalf of fathers or mothers?" she snapped.

"On behalf of parents and families," Belsky shot back.

"NICHD is not willing to get into policy recommendations," responded Friedman, a statement belied by the organization's consistent push for investment in higher-quality day care. "There are other possibilities that can be entertained," she continued, clearly flustered. "Yes, it's a quick solution—more hours [in child care] is associated with more problems. The easy solution is to cut the number of hours but that may have implications for the family that may not be beneficial for the development of the children in terms of economics."

This was the tack initially taken by Belsky's critics in the stories that immediately followed the release of the findings. In an interview right after the press conference, Friedman amplified on this theme by saying that cutting back work hours in order to reduce the hours of child care would likely be unadvisable since the loss of family income and the resulting decline in socioeconomic status would have detrimental effects on children's development. Other day care advocates quickly picked up the tune. "One out of three children whose mothers work would be poor if they didn't work," claimed Helen Blank of the Washington Children's Defense Fund. "Women work for a complex set of reasons. We had national [welfare reform] policy in 1996 that required low-income-level women to work. Many women are working to pay the mortgage or health insurance."[17]

But this response did not challenge the validity of the finding that more hours in nonmaternal care were correlated with behavior problems. Neither did it support the image of fulfilled mothers pursuing careers while their happy children blossom in the hands of competent day care professionals. So Belsky's critics soon changed their strategy to denouncing both the credibility of his explanations and his integrity as a researcher.

An objective witness might have concluded that Belsky's comments at the press conference were rather cautious, given the evidence he had at hand. For example, he did not draw attention to the fact that the correlation found between behavior problems and the amount of time spent in nonmaternal care—regardless of its "quality"—was just as statistically significant as the correlation between behavior problems and two other risk factors already widely acknowledged: poverty and abusive or uncaring parents. In addition, Belsky endorsed two ideas, extended parental leave and flexible work hours, that have long been part of the feminist agenda for "workplace equality." He was also careful not to overstate his conclusions. "I'm not saying they are the super, hyper violent types," he specified. "These kids are more likely to be bullying kids. . . . [W]e are not talking of psychopaths and kids who get guns and blow away other kids."[18]

His restraint won Belsky no credit, however, as the forces of the child care establishment in both the media and the research community went into full damage-control mode, attacking not only his interpretations but his reputation as well.

One theme of this counteroffensive was that the category of "aggressive" behavior was entirely arbitrary, or that the negative connotations associated with "aggressive" were unwarranted and it could actually be viewed positively. "Is it possible that kids are born aggressive, defiant, raring to talk too much at the first opportunity?" asked *Salon* magazine's Jennifer Foote Sweeney, one of Belsky's more aggressive journalistic critics. "There is absolutely no indication that those people have a basis for calling something aggressive; the definition of aggressive behavior is completely nebulous," she claimed on one news program.[19]

"There's no evidence to suggest that an aggressive kindergartener will grow up to be a bully," the *Philadelphia Inquirer* editorialized. "In fact, she might just become a CEO. . . . Also largely overlooked was the good news that children in high-quality day care are academically advanced. . . . Make that a smart, articulate CEO."[20] And *Time* magazine asked,

Should we even be worried at all? The researchers noted that almost all the "aggressive" toddlers were well within the range of normal behavior for four-year-olds. And what about that adjective, anyway? Is a vice not sometimes a form of virtue? Cruelty never is, but arguing back? Is that being defiant—or spunky and independent? "Demanding attention" could be a natural and healthy skill to develop if you are in a room with 16 other kids.[21]

Belsky's critics in the research community echoed the media line. "You could have just as easily called it self-assertion," remarked Harvard professor Kathleen McCartney, one of the principal investigators on the NICHD study.[22] University of Chicago professor Janellen Hutenlocher told the *Chicago Tribune*, "Kids who've spent time in day care certainly learn how to cope socially, and they're certainly much more sturdy little interactors" than those who haven't.[23] Even NICHD director Duane Alexander, facing intense pressure from his researchers to spin the coverage back in a day care–friendly direction, added to the "aggressiveness is good" spin: "Kids push their way in line. They try to get toys from other kids. This is not necessarily pathological."[24] And Sarah Friedman chimed in: "When you use a catchy word like aggression, it's very worrisome. There are words that mean one thing to the scientist who is working on the problem and mean something else in everyday language."[25]

Yet it wasn't merely an issue of mincing words. Perhaps most parents would have agreed that "cruelty," "getting in fights" and "explosive behavior"—three of the measurements used in the study to rate children's behavior—would properly be termed aggressive. More to the point, "aggression" was not an adjective chosen by Belsky, but a clinical term employed by the researchers themselves to indicate disruptive and disobedient, not simply independent and assertive, behavior. The fact that such behavior falls short of "pathological" is hardly reassuring.

A related line of attack centered on the claim that the aggressive behavior recorded among the children with more hours in nonmaternal care was in the "normal" range, and hence not noteworthy. "These behaviors are distributed at the same level in the general population," research team member Susan B. Campbell of the University of Pittsburgh told an interviewer. "These children are completely typical."[26] Jennifer Foote Sweeney likewise averred that "The level of aggression they're talking about is completely normal." She even contended that the children *not* judged aggressive were the abnormal ones: "Children in less child care or no child care are showing much lower levels of aggression that are not considered normal.... [A]pparently [they] don't have skills for dealing with other children. They show an abnormally low percentage of aggression in this study."[27]

Others argued that the 17 percent "aggressive" statistic was not at all remarkable. Dr. Alvin Poussaint, an associate dean at Harvard Medical School, opined that the truly relevant finding of the study was that "83 percent of the children who were in some type of day care did not have these aggressive problems."[28] Researcher Kathleen McCartney told a reporter that "when this measure has been administered to the population at large, 17 percent of all kindergartners" score in the aggressive range. "I'm not saying we should brush these findings away," she added, "but it's totally inaccurate to embrace them and say that child care poses anything of a risk."[29] Edward Zigler, a prominent child development expert at Yale University, argued similarly that "in the normal population of children, that 17 percent is what you find all the time. All those behaviors are within the normal range. This is not clinical pathology we're talking about."[30]

Of course, Belsky never claimed that it was. Moreover, as he later pointed out, the researchers knew that the study sample had a comparatively low proportion of minorities, single-parent families and low-income families—the groups that are already known to account for a disproportionate number of children rated "aggressive." Not only that, but invoking the level of aggression in the general population of children as a benchmark is not particularly meaningful when that population includes large numbers of children who spend extensive hours in day care. The whole point of breaking down the study sample by time spent in day care was to measure the quantitative effects of nonmaternal care in a meaningful way.

The notion that the group of children in question was showing a "normal rate of aggression" seemed to be a deliberate misreading of the study. *All* of the children rated "aggressive" in the study, in fact, showed a degree of aggressive, disobedient behavior that was *not* "within the normal range." Moreover, since observational tests pick up on only the most serious personality problems, already manifesting themselves in behavior, even slight differences are always acknowledged as significant—particularly when they correlate in a "dose-response" fashion to some individual factor, as was the case in this study with regard to numbers of hours in day care. If a substantial percentage of children in day care are exhibiting behavioral problems, many others may be in trouble, although the trouble still lies beneath the surface. Thus, given an observational result of 17 percent of the children with long hours in day care rating as "aggressive," it was not reasonable to infer that the other 83 percent are doing "just fine."

Finally, as Belsky later wrote, the dismissive claim that the observed aggression rate fell "within the normal range" suggested a double standard in light of some of the investigators' previous findings.

> Why have the NICHD study investigators never made it clear that the large majority of children experiencing poor-quality care function "in the normal range"? Why, in fact, when the study found, as it did two years ago, that low-quality care was related to more problem behavior when children were two and three years of age, was there no talk of aggression "in the normal range"? And why is it when higher levels of aggression and disobedience are found to be related to expe-

riences like growing up in poverty or being reared by a depressed mother, that no one ever talks about aggression "in the normal range" as they so cavalierly do now when the issue is the depth of childcare experience?[31]

During an interview in the wake of the controversy, Belsky answered his own question. "Quality of care matters," he agreed, "and so does quantity. The latter part seems to be an intolerable truth."[32]

Some of Belsky's critics flatly contradicted the fact that the study plainly controlled for quality of child care, sensitivity of the mother, poverty and exposure to other children. "Maternal sensitivity is the strongest predictor of behavior problems in children," said Kathleen McCartney. "This effect between hours in care and behavior problems is reduced when we control for maternal sensitivity."[33] Dr. McCartney added a novel twist in another of her attempts to spin the story: "It could be that children with more behavior problems are challenging to their parents and are placed in child care for more hours," she speculated. "It could be that aggression causes more hours [in day care], rather than more hours causing aggression."[34] Incredibly, some argued that the high percentage of children rated "aggressive" in the group with longer hours in day care was meaningless because quality of care was not accounted for. Dr. Zigler of Yale, called "the godfather of child-care research in the United States" by the *Washington Post,* contended that quality was not even part of the study. "That was the piece of that report that was most upsetting to me, because it flies in the face of the evidence," he stated. "Quality does matter. We have study after study proving that." He went on to take a gratuitous swipe at care in the home. "People make the mistake of thinking that home is always great. Home for many kids is no bargain. We have a million abused children, mostly by their parents."[35]

On a talk show about the controversy, child psychiatrists
Alvin Poussaint and John Rosemond also ignored the study's
controls. "I think it probably has something to do with the
quality of daycare and also the parents and their sensibili-
ties and the socioeconomic situation and poverty," Dr. Poussaint said—erroneously on every count. "The fact is," added
Dr. Rosemond, "the researchers here did not differentiate
between types of daycare or quality of daycare. They just
lumped all daycare together."[36]

Some charged that Belsky's research was driven by an
entirely negative, anti–day care agenda. "Belsky is a doom-
sayer who is dismissive of positive findings," asserted Jennifer
Foote Sweeney in *Salon*.[37] His comments about reducing time
in day care were "a 1950s-style attack" on women, according
to Peggy Orenstein.[38] Boston University journalism professor
Caryl Rivers accused Belsky of fomenting "mass hysteria" in
the media about fictional dangers.[39] Even some of Belsky's
fellow researchers on the NICHD study were livid. "I feel we
have been extremely irresponsible, and I'm very sorry the
results have been presented in this way," said the child care
network's lead statistician, Margaret Burchinal.[40] "By not qual-
ifying this, we scared families."[41] Fellow NICHD researcher
Martha Cox of the University of North Carolina said, "He is
more extreme in his views than the rest of us," in yet another
of the slew of interviews given by investigators attempting
to pound Belsky's comments into irrelevance.[42]

Others complained that Belsky's conclusions had not gone
through a proper peer review before he publicized them at
the press conference. "The investigators themselves were not
in agreement as to what the interpretation was," remarked
NICHD director Duane Alexander. "Basically, it was not yet
ready for prime time."[43] But as Belsky pointed out, there had
been no such furor just two years earlier when NICHD
researchers had shared findings generally favorable to day
care, although the research had not been published or peer-

reviewed before being announced to the press. The official NICHD press release in that case, titled "Higher Quality Care Related to Less Problem Behavior" not only made a strong case for a direct relationship between quality of care and behavior, but offered clear policy recommendations as well. As far as proving cause and effect, that is impossible by definition in sociological research, but the "dose-response" relationship Belsky that pointed to is about as close as you can get.

Some of the critical comments made by fellow investigators were unintentionally revealing. "We don't agree with him on his interpretation," colleague Sarah Friedman insisted, characterizing Belsky's comments as "completely unprofessional" to *Salon* magazine. And even if his views differed from the rest of the group, she said, "I thought that, since he was invited to represent the story, he would represent the party line."[44]

TO GET A BETTER GRASP of the "party line," it was necessary only to look at the way Friedman and other NICHD researchers had represented previous research in 1997. That year, the study group reported two major findings: that children in high-quality care showed slightly larger cognitive and linguistic gains than children in poor-quality care; and that the more time children spent in day care, the less affection they showed for their mothers—and the less their mothers showed for them—when they were studied at three years of age. Here's the lead of the official press release: "New research ... indicates that the quality of child care for very young children does matter for their cognitive development and their use of language.... In addition, quality child care in the early years ... can also lead to better mother-child interaction, the study finds." Pages later, buried at the end of the release, the other major finding is alluded to dismissively: "Researchers found that the amount of non-maternal child care was weakly associated with less sensitive and engaged mother-child interaction."[45]

In another paper from the same year, NICHD researchers even implied that women who put their children in day care were psychologically more robust than those who did not. Mothers who returned to work between three and five months after their baby was born were rated "higher on measures of extroversion and agreeableness" and were more likely to use day care. Mothers reluctant to leave their babies were judged to be suffering from "separation anxiety" and were more likely to depend on care by relatives.[46] This amounted to an attempt to portray mothers who felt the need to be with their young children as mentally unstable.

"I sometimes feel I'm in the old Soviet Union," remarked Belsky, "where only certain facts are allowed to be facts, and only certain news is allowed to be news."[47] In unguarded moments, some child development experts have all but admitted that feminist ideology trumps any objective quest for truth when it comes to day care. The study's lead statistician, Margaret Burchinal, acknowledged to the *Los Angeles Times* that she and other researchers had set out to confirm their pro–day care biases.[48] Several years ago, another of Belsky's prestigious colleagues, Dr. Allison Clarke-Stewart of the University of California, acknowledged to a reporter that the research on day care is affected by a hope for agreeable results. "I wanted to find out that child care was good," she said. "I'm a working mother, but that's not the only reason. It made common sense to me."[49] At least Clarke-Stewart can be credited with a degree of candor.

The idea that Belsky had drawn unwarranted conclusions from the newest study's findings might have sounded less hypocritical had his critics refrained from voicing their own conclusions about it, most without a scintilla of evidence. "Hours in care, itself, couldn't possibly explain it," Dr. Friedman insisted, the study's findings notwithstanding. "It's what happens in those hours, or perhaps, what happens at home at the end of the day."[50]

According to his attackers, Belsky was completely out of line in suggesting that parents might consider reducing their use of day care, since institutionalized care is an unalterable fact of modern life. "Child care is a reality in our society for many parents," said Matthew Melmed, a pro–day care lobbyist.[51] "It isn't a question of whether there's going to be day care," claimed Dr. Janellen Huttenlocher of the University of Chicago, "because people's lives today require it. The question is one of how good day care is going to be."[52] Dr. Edward Zigler declared, "Our job isn't to dissuade mothers from using child care by sending up these horror stories. Our real task is to do a public education campaign with parents to get quality care."[53]

All this raises the question of why such an extensive study was carried out in the first place, at considerable taxpayer expense, if so many of the investigators were unwilling to embrace the findings it generated because they contradicted the "party line." For those who have been following the research on day care with a critical eye, nothing in this episode—neither the negative findings nor the ideologically driven reaction—was particularly new. What was different this time around was the media attention given to the public squabbling among sociologists about the meaning of the findings. It's virtually certain that NICHD will do everything in its power to prevent a repeat performance of this embarrassing episode, even if that means imposing new restrictions on researchers and on the release of information to the press.

In fact, soon after the heated battle between Belsky and the phalanx of feminist foes, Duane Alexander announced new restrictive policies at the NICHD designed to prevent future controversies from arising. "There were distortions in the presentations and in the press," he said, promising that "in the future, the group is going to be a lot more careful about how they report their results."[54] When the steering committee of the child care study met in May 2001, Alexander put that promise into action by passing new rules preventing any oral presentation of findings to the media before research has been peer-reviewed.

Several journalists and journalism professors have objected to these restrictions on information despite their own ideological support for day care. Boston University journalism professor Ellen Ruppert Shell said,

> [The restrictions are] not altogether a bad thing. We don't want gadfly social scientists to just put out things. But it has a chilling effect on getting information out to the public. It's putting us in the position of being policed by other professions, and that really diminishes our freedom and our professionalism. It's the information they want us to know.[55]

Sharon Dunwoody, who directs the school of journalism at the University of Wisconsin-Madison, sees similar dangers. "An organization that attempts to control the message, when it's not an evidentiary issue, is simply going to look bad," she argues. "I don't think that works. It's a politically unsavory thing to do." Dunwoody feels that it could even have a chilling effect on the research itself, because it would prevent the "really crucial sharing that needs to go on among scientists."[56]

It seems highly unlikely that complaints about the new restrictions on access to research information will have any effect on NICHD policy, however. It also seems a safe bet that NICHD researchers will help prevent any breaches of protocol (read: outbreaks of candor) in the future. Indeed, they seem to be circling the wagons in support of Alexander's policy. "We cannot take a risk like that again," Sarah Friedman says bluntly.[57] Charles A. Nelson, the University of Minnesota professor of child psychology who served as chair of the SRCD conference, agrees. "To have a press conference elevates early research to a level [to which it] should not be elevated," he says. "The stakes are too high, the policy implications are too great. Science should be cool and objective."[58]

Jay Belsky has his own view about whether day care research is conducted in a "cool and objective" fashion. He says sadly, "I've come to believe that too much of social science research, especially as it gets disseminated, is ideology masquerading as science."[59]

THREE

A Conspiracy of Silence

With all the controversy surrounding the latest child care research, one might think this was the first time that anyone in the field of child development had ever pointed to the detrimental effects of day care on children. In fact, the evidence has been accumulating steadily for decades. That most parents are not aware of this enormous body of evidence is testimony to how successfully day care advocates have controlled the public debate.

Ironically, even the National Institute of Child Health and Human Development (NICHD) has acknowledged in the past that the data point to the likelihood of negative effects from day care. In a review of the existing literature on the subject published in 1996, Michael E. Lamb of NICHD wrote that although day care "need not" be harmful, it often is. Except for the rare situations in which a child in day care has the opportunity to form a strong, stable attachment to one caregiver, Lamb concludes that nonparental care "leads to behavior problems (including aggression and noncompliance)." Previous NICHD reports have also shown deterioration of the mother-child bond with even minimal use of day care by mothers already deemed lacking in sensitivity to their children.[1]

Researchers played down these findings with remarkably dubious logic: since these effects of nonmaternal care were not apparent in children at 15 months, their appearance at 24 and 36 months could not be taken as a reliable indicator of a statistically significant relationship. At the same time, press releases and public statements by NICHD researchers made much of the correlation between the quality of care given to children and their intellectual development. This left the impression that time spent in day care aided learning, even though the "quality of care" in this context referred to how much caregivers talked to their charges one on one, a practice notably absent in the overwhelming majority of day care centers.

These findings on the detrimental effects of day care on behavior and the mother-child bond are merely the latest confirmation of warnings from child development experts over the last forty years—warnings that have been suppressed by the day care establishment. These experts, particularly those specializing in the field of "infant attachment," found conclusive evidence about the dangers of day care for young children long ago. Burton White, former director of the Harvard Preschool Project and a leading authority on the first three years of life, is one of the few who have dared to breach the silence that surrounds this body of research. "After more than thirty years of research on how children develop well," he writes, "I would not think of putting an infant or toddler of my own into any substitute care program on a full-time basis, especially a center-based program." With the exception of short periods of babysitting, White advises parents not to use substitute care at all for the child's first six months, since an infant "has to be responded to intensely during this period." Strictly limited periods of day care are acceptable for children between six months and three years of age, White believes, but he stresses that the child should spend most of his waking hours with a parent or grandparent. "Unless you have a very good reason," he concludes, "I urge you not to delegate the primary child-rearing task to anyone else during your child's first three years of life.... Babies form their first human attachment only once. Babies begin to learn language only once.... The outcomes of these processes play a major role in shaping the future of each new child."[2]

Since many of the critiques of day care for preschoolers depend on an understanding of the concept of infant attachment, it is worth looking back at the recent history of child development theories. In the late 1940s, when the use of formal day care was statistically negligible, it became fashionable among child development experts—in reaction to the "cult of motherhood" decried by Philip Wylie, which had long dominated the popular culture—to hold that babies need only minimal care in the first few years of their development. According to this school of thought, as long as infants and toddlers had the basics of nutrition, hygiene and protection from physical harm, they would thrive with or without doting parents. In terms of their mental and psychological development, infants were regarded as entirely passive, unable to seek out much from their surroundings. A baby's apparent responses to the mother's loving attention were characterized by one scientific curriculum as "a figment of the over-involved mother's imagination, since baby's behavior is random, uncontrolled, essentially autistic." Aside from the physical essentials, it was maintained, all that was needed for proper development was discipline and behavioral conditioning, and these could be provided by any caregiver.[3]

Today the consensus is almost the exact opposite. In light of their research over the past half-century, child development experts now maintain that babies respond to and distinguish various stimuli from birth. The evidence also shows that newborn infants almost immediately establish a strong and irreplaceable relationship with their mothers. Pediatricians Marshall Klaus and John Kennel put it this way: "Detailed studies of the amazing behavioral capacities of the normal neonate have shown that the infant sees, hears, and moves in rhythm to his mother's voice in the first minutes and hours of life."[4] Instead of viewing infants as "passive bundles," child behavior professionals now almost universally recognize that the minds of babies are surprisingly sophisticated.[5]

At the same time that this evolution in thinking about the sensitivity and receptivity of infants was occurring, there were parallel changes in thinking about how interaction with care-givers affected young children. For decades, "attachment the-ory" was widely recognized in child care literature as one of the most important measurements of early child develop-ment. The theory had its origins in England just after World War II, when researchers observed that orphaned and refugee babies "failed to thrive" in excellent institutional care, even if all of their physical needs were met. Some of the babies died with no apparent physical cause. The researchers con-cluded that more than physical care was needed for infants' healthy development: an overriding, dependable attachment to a specific person—usually the mother—who is available to the baby most of the time. Attachment theory posits that the early relationship between infant and caregiver is the foundation of all personality development. The security estab-lished in a stable, nurturing relationship with one person on whom the developing infant can unreservedly depend is, according to this theory, essential in establishing the sense of selfhood and identity necessary for subsequent normal character development. This dependent relationship that the baby forms with one caregiver becomes, paradoxically, the basis for the child's future independence.[6] In the words of one psychologist, "The effect of interrupting attachment bonds during the first two years of life can be a failure to develop a basic trust in constant human relationships with other people."[7]

Children who are "securely attached," according to the theory's original proponents, had the experience in infancy and early childhood of mothers who were readily available, sensitive to their signals, and responsive to their need for comfort and protection.[8] The process of attachment is so important that the relationship formed is the organizing principle of the infant's behavior, psychological states of mind, and even physical development, including seemingly independent processes like heart rate, enzyme levels of growth hormone, and the responsiveness of the immune system.[9]

Since attachment theory originated in the field of psychology, measures of "infant attachment" have sometimes been dismissed as having little hard "scientific" value, particularly by those researchers who prefer the more easily quantifiable measures of intellectual development. But in addition to being widely acknowledged in the field of psychology, measures of infant attachment are among the most reliable barometers of child development across the board. Whether a young child is securely or anxiously attached has proven to be an accurate predictor of school performance, behavior, self-esteem, social competence, and ability to form relationships among other important things.[10]

It is also closely correlated with the likelihood of future mental illness. The population suffering from what psychologists call "antisocial personality disorder" (APD)—those who display psychopathic behavior—accounts for a growing proportion of mentally ill adults in the United States. This group also accounts for a disproportionate amount of aberrant, deviant behavior, including drug abuse, theft and burglary, assault and battery, rape and attempted murder.[11] Symptoms include a pronounced emotional detachment and uncontrollable inner rage, similar to that displayed by the Columbine killers. Psychologists Ken Magid and Carole McKelvey write that "many people with APD began life as unbonded, unattached children. Right now thousands of America's children are in danger of becoming unattached. Well-intentioned parents may be unknowingly placing their young infants at high risk."[12] Magid and McKelvey assert that the "rage and sadness" at the heart of APD have their roots in disrupted early relationships and lack of caregiver consistency.

Perhaps the most dramatic case study testing the validity of attachment theory was the adoption of over eighteen thousand children from Romanian orphanages by couples in the United States after the fall of communism in 1989. Most of these children—deprived of their mothers from infancy— had been confined to cribs much of the time, with a minimal amount of the one-on-one interaction with caretakers that allows personal bonds to develop. The near-universal testimony of the adoptive parents has indicated that these children suffered from an array of physical, emotional, psychological and cognitive problems as a result of their orphanage experience. One study found that 78 percent of the children it evaluated were delayed in motor, social and language skills when they were adopted. They displayed not only cognitive impairments, but also a wide variety of emotional problems, including hypersensitivity to physical touch, violent outbursts, an inability to form bonds with the adoptive parents, distrust of family members combined with alarming effusiveness toward strangers. A *New York Times Magazine* feature on adopted Romanian children concluded that "for a very young child, the lack of an emotional connection with a consistent caretaker can be deeply damaging."[13]

Among the first to make the argument that time in day care puts children at a gravely heightened risk for attachment disorder was the clinician and researcher Selma Frailberg. In her 1977 volume *Every Child's Birthright,* Frailberg made the case that institutional day care, no matter what the quality, is unable to satisfy the need every child has for the devotion of one special adult. Through no fault of their own, says Frailberg, it is impossible for even the best-trained and most highly qualified caregivers in a day care center to treat a particular child as absolutely special. For many preschoolers in purchased care, not only are there long periods when none of the adults present is familiar, but the high turnover of personnel in commercial day care prevents a child from forming a healthy attachment to one caregiver. According to Frailberg, this first leads to sadness in the child, followed by a point where the child ceases to make attachments and to depend on adults in his or her environment. As the years pass, the child is unable to make the lasting commitments and attachments necessary "for love, for trust, for learning and self-worth."[14]

Frailberg's description of how separation affects infants and toddlers is worth quoting at length: "By the time the baby is six months old, love and valuation of his mother take on poignant meaning; even minor separations from her can be distressing"; and "between the ages of six months and three years, children who are strongly attached to their parents will show distress and even panic when they are separated from their parents and left with strangers."[15] Even for older preschoolers, longer periods of nonparental care are harmful:

> When preschool children are separated from their mothers for 9 to 10 hours there is a point of diminishing returns in the nursery day, and finally a point where no educational benefits accrue to the child. By afternoon, after nap time, restlessness, tearfulness, whininess, or lassitude become epidemic in the group of 3 to 6 year olds. Even the most expert teachers have difficulty in sustaining the program and restoring harmony. What we see is longing for mother and home.[16]

While some feminists at the time attacked Frailberg's book as something written "for the 'biology is destiny' fans" and part of an agenda to send women back to home and nursery, her insights were already being confirmed by independent academic studies. The same year in which her book was published saw the release of results from a pilot program at Yale

University designed to offer the best available medical, psychological and social supports to children in the day care setting. In short, it was intended to create the ideal day care environment for healthy development. The reported results were strikingly similar to what Frailberg had described. "Group care," the researchers found, "even under the best circumstances, is stressful for very young children." In contrast to the natural family setting at home, the day care center could only provide "artificial" experiences because it was virtually impossible to duplicate the activities and experiences "most appropriate for the toddler, experiences that he could have at home without anyone giving the matter a moment's thought." Since group care is by nature unsuitable for children under four years of age due to the lack of opportunity to bond with one special adult, children display more obvious signs of stress as the hours in center care grow longer: "Length of day is still very much the issue, for separation reactions become more acute as the day lengthens and fatigue decreases coping ability."[17]

One of the main reasons that center-based day care is not conducive to secure attachment is the turnover and discontinuity of care inherent in any scheme of purchased care. As child development authority Penelope Leach has pointed out, a child in day care regularly has to rely on "somebody who, even if she was there yesterday because it wasn't her day off, doesn't know what happened to that child in the twelve hours previous." Such discontinuity prevents infants from developing a reliable nonverbal language to communicate their needs and emotions to a caregiver who can understand what they are signaling. Discontinuity of care, Leach asserts, has a devastating effect on infants—different only in degree from what was seen in the children from Romanian orphanages:

> The grieving of a baby who loses her one and only special person—her lone mother who dies, for example ... is

agonizing to see because we know we are looking at genuine tragedy. But the pain of the separations we arrange and con- nive at every time we change caregivers or leave a baby in the daycare center that has new staff ... may not be as dif- ferent as we assume.

This is the case, Leach explains, because babies in their first twelve months lack the capacity to understand that the par- ent who leaves is coming back; they have no way of meas- uring the passage of time; and they cannot hold mental images of a missing parent and anticipate that parent's return. Only the adult immediately present can keep the baby "hap- pily afloat."[18]

The other element of commercial care that contributes to attachment disorders, according to researchers, is the dev- astating drop in the sensitivity of caregivers toward individ- ual children in a group care setting. With recent studies showing that half of all preschoolers in day care are moved to different arrangements in the course of one year, that almost half of all caregivers in day care centers quit their positions each year, and that the staff turnover rate has accel- erated sharply over the last decade, these problems are clearly not going away—despite the highest rate of public expen- diture on day care in our history.[19]

EVER SINCE THE LINK BETWEEN day care and attachment dis- order was first noted, the academic left has attacked both the accuracy of the research and the legitimacy of the crite- ria by which the "secure attachment" of young children is assessed. In an argument that foreshadowed the debate over aggressive behavior and day care, prominent University of California psychologist Allison Clarke-Stewart asserted that the seemingly high rate of insecurely attached infants in day care was "within the normal range" of insecure infants found in other countries and hence insignificant. More tellingly, Clarke-Stewart claimed that the categories used to assess attachment were devised by observing children raised at home, and thus were not appropriate for more "independent" day care children. In other words, the completely different character of children in day care rendered them unfit to be judged by standard measures of healthy emotional development—an argument reminiscent of the academic left's dismissal of standardized tests to measure knowledge or intellectual aptitude as inherently "discriminatory" against people with atypical cultural backgrounds.[20]

In recent years, pressure from feminists concerned about the implications of attachment theory for the day care model of childrearing has led to some vigorous backpedaling by some of the theory's most authoritative proponents. For instance, T. Berry Brazelton, author of numerous popular works on child development who is often identified as America's leading pediatrician, repeatedly expressed his concerns about early extended separation of infants and toddlers from their mothers. In his 1969 bestseller, *Infants and Mothers,* he suggested that early separation should be avoided whenever possible. Five years later, in another popular book, *Toddlers and Parents,* he warned that such separation could have seriously detrimental effects on children, relating the plight of a disturbed and withdrawn young girl by way of example. In the most recent edition of *Infants and Mothers,* however, Brazelton not only drops the strong advice about avoiding early separation, but apologizes for any offense he may have given working mothers: "Inadvertently I may have added to mothers' feelings of guilt when they were not able to stay at home throughout the first year. This has not been my intent, for I have seen how critical it was to many young women to include a job in their daily lives." Brazelton's withdrawal of his previous admonitions is not based on any new evidence calling into question the correlation between day care and attachment disorders in children; he simply fears offending some parents by mentioning inconvenient facts.[21]

Another attachment advocate who recanted in the face of feminist pressure is Dr. Benjamin Spock. For most of his long and influential career, Spock advised mothers with children under four years of age to stay home with them as much as possible. At one time, he was unambiguously opposed to infant day care, saying that "a day nursery . . . is no good for an infant. There's nowhere near enough attention or affection to go around." Since children need full-time love and attention in their early years, he argued, it is senseless for parents to "pay other people to do a poorer job of bringing up their children." As late as 1977, he was still saying that "if a mother realizes clearly how vital this kind of care is to a small child it may make it easier to decide that the extra money she may earn . . . is not so important after all." But after years of taking heat from feminists, Dr. Spock altered his emphasis considerably. In the 1992 edition of his classic *Baby and Child Care* there is nary a word about the importance of infant-mother attachment, and he explicitly contradicts his earlier counsel to mothers. "Parents who know that they need a career or a certain kind of work for fulfillment," he writes, "should not give it up for the sake of the children. Instead, I think such parents should work out some kind of compromise between their two jobs and the needs of their children, usually with the help of other caregivers, especially during the crucial first three years of a child's development." Two years later, in *A Better World for Our Children: Rebuilding American Values,* Dr. Spock casually suggests that "it is particularly desirable" for parents to spend time with children during the first three years—a far cry from his original insistence that mothers being with their children "as much as possible" during these crucial years is a "necessity." Spock has explained his change of phrasing with surprising candor:

I'm scared of going out too strongly for "You should stay home!" because in early editions of *Baby and Child Care* I hinted at that by saying "the early years are very crucial, and maybe you should postpone the advantages of earning a living." And women pounced on me, [saying,] "You made me feel very guilty!" But I noticed they went off to work anyway even if they felt guilty, and that's . . . the worst of all possible arrangements. So I just tossed it. It's a cowardly thing that I did; I just tossed it in subsequent editions.[22]

Even some of those advocates of attachment theory who remain firmly committed to the importance of one-on-one care for infants and toddlers have done some backtracking in recent years. Penelope Leach, famous for her association with attachment theory, remains an opponent of institutional care for children less than eighteen months of age. But in her 1994 book, *Children First,* there is not only a shift in perspective away from the developmental needs of children toward the emotional and financial needs of parents, but also a move away from her longtime defense of at-home mothering. "The necessity for full-time exclusive mothering," Leach writes, "has been exposed as a myth of the postwar West." And because society has so devalued parenting, she suggests that "individual good parenting is not only exceedingly difficult but, ultimately, insufficient"—a message that seems tailored to feminist critics who accused Leach of feeding culturally conditioned and unnecessary guilt by setting expectations too high.

The popular literature on childrearing has undergone a marked shift in the past decade by accommodating feminists' insistence that day care is an unalterable "fact" of modern life because of both economic necessity and parents' needs for autonomy. Indeed, the shift away from attachment theory has been much more pronounced than the examples I have given indicate, since authorities like Leach, Spock and Brazelton still lean generally toward explanations of early child development that stress the primary importance of parents spending time with children. For many others, parent-child "bonding" (a word that has displaced "attachment" in much of the literature) is described as a rather cursory experience, suited to the on-the-go lifestyle of the dual-career couple. In one guide, *What to Expect the First Year,* parents are advised that "bonding can take three months," or in special cases such as a baby with colic, slightly longer. Other books claim that successful bonding can be accomplished within the infant's first weeks, days or even hours. The most extreme example of the time necessary for a healthy infant-parent bond may be the "thirty to forty-five minutes" recommended by Tracy Hotchner in *Pregnancy and Childbirth.* After this speedy attachment, presumably, mom can devote herself to more important things without worrying overmuch about junior's well-being.[23]

For years, academic feminists in the field of child development have reassured dual-career couples that putting an infant or toddler in day care would have no damaging effects, despite apparent indications to the contrary. Now these social scientists insist that day care is actually *better* for young children than home care. The children of working mothers, writes Anna Shreve in her study of modern family life, *Remaking Motherhood,* may enjoy various benefits including "a higher I.Q.," "better social adjustment," "more expansive sex-role ideology, greater self-esteem, greater confidence in one's abilities, a more positive view of women, better educational progress, more vocational options, and a potential for greater economic independence." According to Susan Faludi, "If day care has any long-term effect on children ... it seems to make [them] slightly more gregarious and independent."[24] One of the foremost opponents of attachment theory, psychologist Diane Eyer, even argues that the parental influence on children is overstated. "Children are profoundly affected by an array of people who interact with them," she writes, "by the foods they eat, by the music they hear, by the television they watch, by the hope they see in the adult world and by the institutions—especially schools—they attend."[25]

This downgrading of the parental role's importance has reached the extent of celebrating the independence of latch-key children. In *The Way We Never Were,* which argues that the stable nuclear family of bygone days has been overly sentimentalized, Stephanie Coontz points out that "studies in Philadelphia and the South showed latch-key children performing equally well with others in school. Researchers also have noted positive effects of self-care on children's sense of self-discipline and responsibility." Incredibly, among the positive effects claimed by Coontz is the "healthier and better adjusted" personalities of adolescents who have experimented with drugs.

The movement away from attachment theory in popular guides for parents and the celebration of the independence-building potential of day care for preschoolers appear to be wishful thinking on a grand scale. Because the "new life script" for the modern mother requires her to remain steadily on the career track in uninterrupted competition for economic as well as social and political equality, she must not have to worry that these healthy aspirations will have ill effects on her children. But studies over the last few decades have provided no grounds for dismissing fears about the potentially detrimental impact of heavy reliance on day care. On the contrary: the evidence regarding our vast and unprecedented experiment in proxy parenting indicates that the breezy reassurances given to moms by feminist academics are unwarranted.

EXPERTS HAVE BEEN AWARE of a consistent link between time in day care and attachment disorders as well as aggressive behavior for many years now. Researchers at the University of Illinois concluded in 1987 that infants left in day care because of full-time maternal employment were more likely to avoid or ignore their mothers after a short separation than were infants cared for at home, a pattern of "insecure-avoidant" behavior that suggests a significant deterioration of the bond between infant and mother.[26] A paper published the following year in the *Journal of Child Psychology and Psychiatry* found a "robust" association between extensive day care begun before age one and insecure mother-child relationships.[27] Another study by researchers at the University of California in 1992 found that children feel significantly less secure with their caregivers in day care centers than they do with their mothers, no matter how consistent the out-of-home care is.[28] A broad-based international analysis by scholars at the University of Calgary involving over 22,000 children observed that almost 50 percent of children in day care had an insecure attachment to their mothers, and concluded that "full-time care for infants and young children [in day care puts] a substantial proportion of the population at risk for psychological maladaptation."[29] Similarly, an analysis done for the U.S. Department of Health and Human Services in 1991—even while trying to downplay the finding by stating that "most babies with employed mothers are securely attached to them"—said that 45 percent of infants of mothers employed full-time were insecurely attached. Using the report's own numbers, this meant a 55 percent higher risk of insecure attachment compared with children of mothers not employed full-time.[30]

There are early indications that the disruptions of the infant-mother bond correlated with extended time in day care have long-lasting psychological effects. A recent study of medical students identified a clear link between poor attachment in childhood and high levels of loneliness, depression, anxiety, low self-esteem and inability to deal with difficulties in adulthood.[31] These findings corroborate the trends that psychologists are seeing in their professional practice. Stanford University psychologist Bryna Siegel has noted that "clinician colleagues are reporting an increase in the number of children with unstable, extensive daycare histories in their practices." An article several years ago in the *Journal of the American Psychoanalytic Association* reported that among "patients with an early history of surrogate mothering," there was a significant pattern of "estrangement from biological mothers, and intolerance of intimate relationships."[32]

These academic case studies merely reflect information that is common knowledge to practicing clinical psychologists. In his book *Becoming Attached,* Robert Karen states that psychologists now know that "a certain style of mothering— warm, sensitive, responsive, and dependable"—fosters emotional well-being. "Insecure" or "anxious" infant-mother attachment can "reverberate through the child's life in the form of lowered self-esteem, impaired relationships, inability to seek help or to seek it in an effective way, and distorted character development." Infants who are insecurely attached to their mothers, according to Karen, are likely to grow up as "aggressive defiant children" or as "clingy, panicky children" who later in life may be "lacking in self-reliance . . . and plagued by insecurity in [their] relationships." In extreme cases, "early ambivalent attachment may be a contributing factor . . . [to] the borderline personality" that manifests itself in "impulsive, self-destructive, and rageful" conduct. According to Karen, psychologists have firmly established that "insecure attachment, which shows up at twelve months, is predictive of behavior not only at three, five, seven or fourteen years . . . but also at twenty, thirty, and seventy, as people make romantic choices, parent their own children, get into marital squabbles, and face the loneliness of old age." Many psychologists assume as a matter of course that children placed in day care full-time in the first year will grow

up to be "first-graders who [are] more difficult, argumenta-
tive, and aggressive—hitting, kicking, swearing, shoving:
and nine- and ten-year-olds who [are] seen as more troubled
by their peers."[33]

Karen's blunt appraisal of the psychological fallout from
nonmaternal care indicates part of the trouble with the assaults
on attachment theory. Critics would have us believe that
measures of attachment and its consequences are too amor-
phous to meet the strict "scientific" criteria that would make
them a useful tool in assessing true risks to healthy development. But they fail to acknowledge that the way in which
children learn self-control—unlike motor skills or other secondary abilities—is a psychological process of internalizing
moral requirements by a complex system of cultivation, modeling, understanding, approval and disapproval. And it seems
that the way this system develops is through consistent,
devoted, individualized care. This helps to explain why children who spend long hours in day care are inclined to be
more "aggressive" and "noncompliant": their moral sensibil-
ities have been stunted by the lack of "attachment" to one
special adult, a prerequisite for internalizing a moral code.

Dr. Stanley Greenspan alludes to this difficulty in his recent
book *The Four-Thirds Solution.* "It's difficult at present," he
writes, "to sufficiently measure many of the most important
emotional capacities, such as the depth of a child's capacity
for intimacy, her sense of self, and her future capacities to
parent and nurture children as well as pursue a career." Our
current methods, he argues, are adequate "only to scratch
the surface ... and gauge some 'measurable' aspects of social
competence." According to Greenspan, many other important social, emotional and intellectual abilities influenced
by early childhood experiences don't manifest themselves
until adulthood.[34] Poorly attached children are, in many
ways, ticking time bombs that only give faint clues to the
devastation they will later wreak on themselves and others.

But even if they are faint, the clues are abundant. As far as aggressive behavior goes, here too the recent studies simply underscore a long history of findings. As early as 1974, *Developmental Psychology* reported that three- and four-year-olds who had been put in day care in their first year of life were more physically and verbally abusive with adults and peers, less cooperative and less tolerant of frustration than their home-reared counterparts. A 1988 paper by Dr. Edward Zigler (the same Dr. Zigler who would publicly attack Jay Belsky fourteen years later for saying essentially the same thing) stated that "from the research carried out to date, a tentative consensus emerges that ... children who have experienced early group care tend towards assertiveness, aggression, and peer rather than adult orientation."[35] One study from the University of North Carolina concluded that kindergarteners and first graders who had been placed in the "extremely high quality daycare center" run by the university in their first year were more likely to "hit, kick and push" as well as "threaten, swear and argue" than their at-home counterparts. These children were described by teachers as having "a serious deficit in social behavior."[36] Another study from Texas found that a history of extensive day care was a good predictor of eight-year-olds receiving low ratings from teachers in the areas of compliance, work habits, peer relationships and emotional health. These children also earned lower grades for classes and conduct and were more difficult to discipline. The negative effects were not diminished by a higher quality of care.[37]

There are some preliminary indications that these behavioral problems may be related to the unnaturally stressful environment that preschoolers are subjected to in center-based care. A little-discussed article published several years ago in *Child Development* provided medical evidence for this theory. Researchers at the University of Minnesota were astonished to find that the levels of cortisol, a chemical indicating stress, rose during the day for children in day care. Normally, cortisol levels start high in the morning and taper off in the afternoon. The "remarkable and unexpected" discovery that this pattern was "exactly reversed" among children in day care has child psychologists worried.[38] According to Dr. Stanley Greenspan, "the long-term effects of these rises in cortisol" in terms of "disordered functioning" have yet to be determined. "But this study raises questions about the degree of stress that toddlers and preschoolers experience in all-day group day-care settings."

One source of stress for preschoolers in day care may be the clash between parental and "professional" approaches to discipline. Writing in the seventies, before such blunt appraisals became a thing of the past in social science departments, Harvard psychologists Jerome Kagan, Richard Kearsley and Philip Zelazo said that "many day care workers, trained in a philosophy of permissiveness toward aggression and emotional spontaneity, are reluctant to punish every misdemeanor. . . . The parent with an articulated idea and coherent philosophy of child rearing . . . might view the day care environment as dangerously indifferent" to behavior he or she would not accept at home.[39]

The dirty little secret of the attachment theory critics is that behavioral studies since the late 1960s have shown precisely what the theory's proponents predicted from the beginning: a significant correlation between time in day care and problem behavior. No matter how much they downplay the statistical importance of the findings or nitpick over the definition of words like "aggressive" or "abnormal," the link has shown up in study after study for thirty years. Even Allison Clarke-Stewart, one of Jay Belsky's outspoken adversaries, has admitted that the findings show day care kids to be "less polite, less agreeable, less respectful of others' rights, more irritable, more rebellious [and] more aggressive with their peers."[40] Her disagreement with Belsky seems to be over whether such behavior is anything to worry about. Indeed, she has argued that these characteristics indicate an admirably independent spirit. "Children who have been in day care," she wrote in 1989, "think for themselves [and] want their own way. . . . They are not willing to comply with adults' arbitrary rules."[41] While Clarke-Stewart makes a mighty effort to redefine virtuous behavior, most parents would not agree that the behavior she describes above is in any way desirable.

In fact, the notion that "independence" and "assertiveness" in small children might be virtues that give them a step up in life has been largely debunked. A 1990 study from the Institute of Human Development at the University of California found that it was those who had been judged "dependent in childhood" who emerged as adults "with a quite distinctive catalog of impressive attributes . . . calm, warm, giving, sympathetic, insightful, undefensive, incisive, consistent across roles, comfortable with ambiguity and uncertainty, and socially poised."[42] Psychologist Anan Sroufe observed that young children who were securely attached as infants were actually "more ego resilient, independent, compliant, empathic and socially competent" than were those who were poorly attached. While day care advocates constantly tout the advantages of "socialization" that center-based care provides to infants and toddlers, a study published several years ago in the *Child Study Journal* found that, contrary to the expectations of the researchers, one-year-olds with little or no day care experience consistently behaved more "prosocially" than their peers with more day care experience. The conclusion: that "the only significant predictor of prosocial behavior" was a *lack* of day care experience.[43]

WHAT ABOUT THE BENEFITS in cognitive development that day care supposedly confers on children? Even if day care has been shown to be a serious risk factor for social and emotional growth, don't the advantages for intellectual growth balance out the downsides?

On closer inspection, the putative advantage for children's mental development also turn out to be an illusion. While defenders of day care for preschoolers point to supposed gains in areas such as vocabulary and short-term memory brought by the "intellectually stimulating" environment of a group care setting outside the home, there is actually no evidence that such benefits are conferred by day care. In fact, the massive effort to cast day care for infants and toddlers as an advantageous component of early preparation for learning in school is a deception.

Much of the enormous amount of attention given to the "crucial first three years of brain development" has centered on the notion that a formal, systematic "educational" setting like a day care center is best able to provide the mental stimulation that babies and toddlers need during this formative stage. What the research actually shows is that "quality of care"—here referring to how much caregivers talk to their charges—is what correlates to cognitive development, not center-based care per se. And in light of the poor quality of care offered in most existing day care centers, the experience is likely to be an intellectual *risk* for infants and toddlers.[44] One study frequently cited by day care advocates as proof of the "enriched" intellectual environment of early day care involves the Carolina Abecedarian Project. According to this study, low-income, at-risk children in the preschool program benefited slightly over at-risk kids not in the program. But even in this high-risk group, the benefits were quite modest: 30 percent of the children participating in the program still had to repeat a year of school, and their I.Q. scores were just five points higher than those of children not participating. Children in the program still performed far worse than the average child.[45]

Such dubious use of studies to argue in favor of more government investment in day care is commonplace. In some ways, the whole propaganda effort surrounding babies' brain development in the first three years is part of this strategy. Actor-director Rob Reiner's I Am Your Child Foundation has spent millions on advertising that uses simple studies showing how the brains of animals do not develop properly if deprived of stimulation during critical periods of their infancy as a way of arguing that children will be "hard-wired" to succeed in school if their parents put them in "enriched" day care environments when they are infants. But the animal studies only show, at most, that traits common to an entire species fail to develop when the brain is deprived of stimulation. Any further conclusion as to the benefits of early day care for brain development is a rather large leap of imagination—but one that is regularly accepted by the media.

In fact, quality of day care accounts for very little of the measurable differences in academic performance and cognitive development among children. According to John Bruer's *The Myth of the First Three Years,* only 1 to 4 percent of these differences have anything to do with the quality of outside-the-home care, while 96 to 99 percent are attributable to the influence of parents.[46] This has been known for many years: a federally funded study in the 1970s found that "the most important determinant of education attainment is family background."[47] As education analyst Lawrence Steinberg has written, most of the problems related to poor academic performance can be traced to "the disengagement of parents and a peer culture that demeans academic performance."[48] One would think this might inspire policies designed to help parents spend more time with and become more engaged with their children rather than provide incentives for parent-child separation. But the day care lobby in Washington has considerably more influence than parents.

There are other indications that day care actually retards intellectual development. One study in England, for example, found that six-year-olds with extensive day care histories had lower language skills than peers raised at home. (This discovery was even more surprising to researchers in that the group of day care children studied were of a higher socioeconomic status on average than the at-home group.)[49] In 1986, sociologist J. Conrad Schwartz found that group care was "associated with lower intelligence, poorer verbal skills and shorter attention."[50] A University of Missouri study from 1991 found that "no day care in infancy was the best predictor of above average high school achievement."[51] Another study from the same year found that third-graders who had been placed in day care as preschoolers had lower grades and demonstrated poorer study skills, concluding that extensive day care experience was "the single best predictor (in a negative direction) of ratings by parents, teachers and peers and of report card grades and standardized test scores."[52]

It is likely that the cognitive problems reflected in these studies result from a lack of interaction between mother and child. An extensive survey published by the National Bureau of Economic Research suggests that children's educational achievement can be held back significantly if their mothers work full-time. According to Christopher Ruhm, an economist at the University of North Carolina who analyzed the survey, three- and four-year-olds tended to have lower verbal ability if their mothers worked during the child's first year, while five- and six-year-olds showed poorer reading and math skills if their mothers worked during any of the child's first three years. The type of outside-the-home care used by working parents did not seem to have affected the outcomes.[53]

A big influence on the view that day care provides an "enriched" learning environment that can aid the intellectual development of preschoolers has been the purported successes of the Head Start program in giving underprivileged children an academic step up. But available research casts doubt on government efforts to improve academic performance by putting preschoolers in nonparental care. At best, Head Start may help children who are the most economically disadvantaged; but even this has been called into question. One study showed that Head Start children, compared with disadvantaged children who had no preschool at all, scored "lower on almost all measures [upon entering school]."[54] And while some research indicates educational advantages from short daily periods of nursery school for three- to five-year-olds, it is completely misleading to compare this to long hours in a day-nursery. According to many experts, the educational benefits of a group setting for children under four years of age are nonexistent.

THE MOST DAMNING EVIDENCE of all concerning the dangers of day care involves health risks, sometimes grave, that group care presents for small children. The drastically elevated incidence of infectious disease among day care children is hardly a secret among pediatricians and epidemiologists. The problem surfaced in dramatic form a decade ago when *Pediatric Annals* devoted a special issue to day care–related diseases, headlining their lead editorial, "Day Care, Day Care: Mayday! Mayday!"[55] The statistics are truly shocking. According to one estimate published by the American Academy of Family Physicians, children in day care are eighteen times more likely to become ill than other children; at any one time, 16 percent of those attending day care are likely to be sick. (Of those sick children, 82 percent continue to attend day care in spite of their illness.)[56] Day care children are anywhere between three and four-and-a-half times more likely to be hospitalized than those raised at home.[57] One study estimated that "children in day care are at a 50 percent to 100 percent increased risk for contracting [certain] fatal and maiming diseases for each year in day care."[58]

The illnesses and infections rampant in the group care setting range from mild to very serious. Infants in day care, for instance, have almost twice the rate of inner ear infections as infants raised at home.[59] The incidence of respiratory illness is also much higher in day care centers: 100 percent higher for infants and 25 to 50 percent higher for older preschoolers than for their counterparts at home.[60] And that is just the average. For one respiratory illness—pneumococcal disease—the risk of infection is *36 times higher* among children under two in day care than it is among children cared for in the home.[61]

The incidence of hemophilus influenza type B is twelve times higher for children in day care; infection rates for giardiasis (a type of diarrhea) fifteen to twenty times higher.[62] Some illnesses transmitted with disturbing frequency in day care are very serious indeed, and are often spread from day care centers to the community at large. ("Children in day care are responsible for many community disease outbreaks," reports an article in *American Family Physician*.)[63] According to the American Academy of Pediatrics, bacterial meningitis and hepatitis A occur at much higher rates in day care centers; 50 percent of day care centers that admit children under two experience outbreaks of hepatitis A.[64] Public health officials have speculated that "day care centers may represent the major source of hepatitis A cases of uncertain origin" (more than 60 percent of all cases).[65] Experts have characterized death rates from Sudden Infant Death Syndrome (SIDS) as "disproportionately high" in day care centers, and are puzzled by the fact that the demographic characteristics of these SIDS victims—white, born to older, more educated parents, without a history of exposure to smoke—would normally put them in the lowest risk category.[66]

Even some less serious illnesses can have serious compli-
cations. By age two, 22 percent of young children in day care
centers have contracted chronic inner ear infections (*otitis
media*) that require the surgical placement of drainage tubes
in the inner ear, while only 3 percent of children in home
care require such treatment. Experts worry about such high
rates of inner ear infection, not only because of the risks
entailed in surgery but also because the mild hearing loss
that frequently results can hinder psychological and social
development.[67] And even though the high incidence of the
cytomegalovirus (CMV) found in day care centers doesn't
pose a grave risk to the preschoolers that contract it, CMV
does present very serious dangers to unborn children who
may be exposed to a significantly elevated risk of CMV-related
birth defects affecting vision, brain development, hearing
and neuromuscular functioning.[68]

French scholars have characterized the process of outbreak
and spread of disease in group day care as similar to what
was found in orphanages in previous ages.[69] One prominent
medical researcher says that day care is responsible for "outbreaks of enteric illness—diarrhea, dysentery, giardiasis, and
epidemic jaundice—reminiscent of the pre-sanitation days
of the seventeenth century."[70] In 1991, an epidemiologist
termed day care centers "the open sewers of the twentieth
century."[71]

It appears that the high rate of disease transmission in day
care centers is unrelated to the "quality" of the center, but is
simply a function of bringing large numbers of infants and
toddlers together in the same facility. One medical authority
has remarked that in an environment where diaper changing is the main activity and a typical day care child puts a
hand or some other object in his mouth every three minutes,
"there seem to be few specific actions to be taken" to prevent
the transmission of disease.[72] Government regulation has
done nothing to help the situation. The Centers for Disease

Control has warned that even "large, licensed day care centers ... are major transmission centers for hepatitis, severe diarrhea, and other diseases."[73]

One particularly worrisome aspect of these health matters is what pediatric researchers have recently called "one of the most important public health issues of the decade"—the massive overprescription of antibiotics.[74] The medical community is enormously concerned that as antibiotics are prescribed in more and more cases where they are not medically indicated, germs and pathogens are mutating into strains that resist antibiotic treatment. Analyzing the 192 percent increase in the number of prescriptions written for one antibiotic used to treat inner ear infections, medical authorities concluded that it was "due in part to widespread day care attendance, improved access to care, and overprescription of antimicrobial agents."[75] And the problem does not result simply from an attempt to protect children from the disease-ridden environment of the day care center; much of it is due to *parental dependence* on the day care regime. A survey of pediatricians confirmed that 96 percent of them had received requests from parents to prescribe antibiotics to their children when they were not medically indicated; one-third admitted to "complying with these requests."[76] In explanation of this phenomenon, one pediatrician involved in a study several years ago said bluntly that "my patients' parents ... want to be able to get the child back to day care quickly."[77]

The problem is so serious that some experts believe that "efforts to reduce antibiotic use in children should be particularly directed toward young children in day care centers."[78] But such efforts seem to have little chance of success. A widely reported recent study showed that public health campaigns aimed at doctors and parents lowered rates of antibiotic prescriptions for children across the board—except for those in day care. Researchers found "no significant

impact" on either antibiotic use or the incidence of resistant bacteria among children in day care, prompting the
author of the study to conclude that "we need more effective strategies to promote appropriate antibiotic use for children in day care."[79]

Although the heavy use of antibiotics in hospitals is usually cited by news stories as the primary factor, hospitals are
"not solely to blame for today's worrisome increase in antibiotic-resistant bacteria," one science writer reports. "Experts
also point to day care centers as prime 'clearinghouses' for
spreading antibiotic-resistant infections."[80] Unlike hospital
patients, children in day care carry these drug-resistant bugs
outside the institutional environment when they come home
every evening, and physicians are concerned that "children
congregating in day care centers pass on resistant bugs to
each other and later to their families and society at large."[81]

Physicians speculate that another factor in the increased
susceptibility to disease exhibited by children in day care
may be that their immune systems are deficient from lack
of breastfeeding. Precisely because epidemiological research
demonstrates that breastfeeding of infants significantly
decreases the risk for a large number of acute and chronic
diseases—including diarrhea, respiratory infection, inner
ear infection, meningitis and even Sudden Infant Death Syndrome—the American Academy of Pediatrics (AAP) recommends that infants be breastfed for at least the first year of
life. In the United States currently, only 21 percent of mothers are nursing at six months, and many of these are supple-
menting with formula.[82] Although statistics are unavailable
for infants in extended day care, the breastfeeding rates for
this group are clearly far lower. While the AAP has made the
promotion of breastfeeding one of its major efforts because
of the "health, nutritional, immunological, developmental,
[and] psychological" benefits it brings both infants and mothers, progress is unlikely given that the percentage of women

going back to work soon after giving birth continues to go up, as does the use of commercial day care.[83]

Given all the evidence showing that day care is a petri dish for disease, the dearth of public discussion about the health dangers of center-based care for infants and toddlers is hard to fathom. Perhaps one reason for this silence is that the studies related to the transmission of disease are found primarily in medical journals, while studies of day care per se are mostly in advocacy articles in sociological journals. Another reason may be the almost complete absence of news media attention. The only major coverage of the issue in the past years consisted of some excited reports about the health *benefits* of day care.

In August of 2000, after the *New England Journal of Medicine* published an article noting that children who attended day care in their first six months were less likely to develop asthma later in childhood, the *New York Times* headlined "Day Care, for Keeping Asthma at Bay" and the *Washington Post* front-paged the story with the headline "Day Care May Boost Immunity to Asthma." But in their haste to report positive research related to day care, both papers got it badly wrong. It turned out that the study actually indicated that regular contact with other children boosted immunity to asthma, whether it was siblings and playmates at home or other children in day care. And since other studies have consistently pointed out that increased use of day care has been involved in the doubling of childhood asthma over the last twenty years, "positing a cause-and-effect relationship between day care and *reduced* asthma faces a formidable hurdle," in the words of David Murray of the Statistical Assessment Service. Murray went to the trouble of doing a newspaper database search for coverage of two other recent studies, both showing an association between the use of day care and increased incidence of serious respiratory infections. One of the major studies received no coverage at all; the other was mentioned in passing in exactly one newspaper story. The huge disparity between the noncoverage of these stories and the avalanche of glowing reports that greeted the supposedly "positive" asthma finding, Murray speculated, was probably due to the fact that "many in the media, along with a growing proportion of the population, are working parents plagued by the problem of caring for children. Hence, there may be pressures to ignore studies that contradict our desires, while studies that reinforce them are assigned greater importance."[84]

As we have seen, the vast majority of "working parents plagued by the problem of caring for children" are very uncomfortable with the decision to put their children in day care; they seek to avoid center-based care when at all possible; and they would stay home with their children themselves if they felt it were a financially viable option. They would probably be even more uncomfortable with the day care option if they knew the truth about the developmental and health risks they are subjecting their kids to when they drop them off every morning.

FOUR

The Day Care Establishment

With all the reasons to be concerned about institutional day care for young children, and with the amount of discomfort that parents themselves express about out-of-home care for their children (and their desire to spend more time rearing them at home), why do government and corporate policies favor the one child care option—commercial day care—that most parents wish to avoid? Why is there no robust debate about this revolutionary experiment in childrearing? And, the most important question of all, if parents, children and our society at large do not benefit from the growing regime of institutionalized and government-subsidized day care, who does?

Qui bono? is a question rarely asked in this debate. The truth is that the public discussion regarding how we ought to rear our children as well as public and business policies related to child care are controlled by a relatively small group of reporters, sociologists, corporate managers and professional day care interest groups. This day care establishment jealously guards its domination of the public discussion, and works to shut down any dissent from its agenda: establishing institutionalized day care for young children as a social norm, whether most parents like it or not.

Most directly influential in controlling the public debate about this vital matter are, of course, the news media. Not only does the press establish the boundaries of socially acceptable opinion on the subject of day care, but it also controls the access that parents have to the crucial information about day care necessary to make informed decisions about its use. And almost without exception, day care is cast in a positive light—not just as a responsible choice, but as the best possible choice for enlightened parents. Media coverage of day care is one-sided and riddled with conflicts of interest.

This truth was recognized years ago in *A Mother's Work,* a perceptive book by Deborah Fallows that still stands as the best firsthand account of the realities of center-based child care. The book offers a chilling portrait of what children experience in the typical group care setting: boredom and regimented activities; impatient staffers endlessly seeking diversions for children wondering when their parents will return; little individual attention or special instruction and little affection; sick toddlers; and such a lack of "continuous care" that the names of the children are often forgotten. One passage from the book summarizes what Fallows encountered:

> The teacher watching the twenty-seven children tried her hardest, ad-libbing her way from one activity to the next. She put on a record and started to dance. One little blond boy started dancing along with her. A few others joined the group. Five or six gathered by some swinging cabinet doors that formed the partition between the play area and the rest of the room. One little girl sat by herself, crying softly in the corner. The rest wandered around. For about eight seconds the music played and the children danced. Then a fight erupted between two little boys, and the teacher had to stop dancing to break it up. Without her example, the dancing died off. She tried again a few minutes later but was interrupted this time by a small couple who tripped over each other. Again, the dancers stopped. She gave up records then and tried reading a story. The same few eager dancers moved right in to listen, while the rest kept on swinging on the cabinet doors or aimlessly wandering. The little girl was still crying in her corner. After

a short story, the teacher opened the large cabinet and pulled
out some puppets. They immediately attracted the largest
crowd of the morning. All but a few rushed right over to watch
the show. But the brilliance of the idea dimmed after several
moments. As her impromptu story line weakened, the toddlers drifted back to their swinging doors and wandering,
shuffling their feet, chasing back and forth.[1]

As to why this depressing environment is never pictured in
the literature about day care, Fallows explains that "[belief]
in day care as an institution" has become a tenet of faith for
feminists, and therefore "criticism of day care has become
... a taboo." But, in many ways, this applies only to the
united front that must be maintained in public to preserve
the victories of the women's movement with regard to
women in the workplace:

> People may be willing to entertain private, among-friends
> complaints about the defects or costs of certain centers or cer-
> tain approaches, as long as everyone understands that they
> all believe in day care as an institution. But when the criti-
> cism is conducted in public, where the gains by the women's
> movement still seem so fragile, can it be anything but a hos-
> tile act? It is but a short step from criticizing day care to sug-
> gesting that there might be fundamental conflicts between
> parenthood and career.

Fallows thinks that this mentality also goes far toward
explaining the "no-bad-news" line of many journalists on
the issue of day care. She gives the example of a 1983 column by Ellen Goodman that took offense at a warning by
the American Medical Association that day care centers were
becoming breeding grounds for infectious disease. Goodman
argued that by focusing on the "relatively minor problems"
of the day care system, doctors ignored the *real* problem,
which was "those who don't have access" to day care at all.

Fallows regards Goodman as exemplifying the worldview that "seem[s] to think that acknowledging day care's defects is too grave a political risk even to be contemplated."[2] Twenty years later, Goodman is still writing columns reflecting the same views. In the wake of the latest dispute over the connection between day care and aggressive behavior in children, she advises working mothers to "take your dose of research with a large chaser of skepticism" in order to avoid "a case of gut wrench and guilt sweats."[3] The latter phrase says it all.

Sometimes the reluctance on the part of the press to confront the negative evidence results in distorted coverage. The PBS network produced a television documentary in 1991, entitled *Childhood,* about the evolution in theories of child development, which included an excerpt from René Spitz's classic film on the damaging effects of maternal deprivation, a film that had an enormous effect on an entire generation of child development experts. In the PBS documentary, the Spitz film was used simply as a brief example of how unwarranted estimates of the importance of maternal care had deformed early research on child development. No mention was even made that early mother-child separation was a proven cause of alarm in childrearing.[4]

The unwillingness to admit to any problems with the day care model of parenting sometimes takes the form of outright censorship of anything even hinting that it is a contentious issue for working moms. When Felice Schwartz suggested in a *Harvard Business Review* article that companies might institute a dual-track system for female employees—one for childless women or those mothers comfortable with putting their children in day care, and another for working moms who want to spend more time with their children (an idea later derisively termed the "Mommy Track")—most of those in the media who didn't attack the idea as retrograde simply refused to discuss it. Editors at magazines like

Working Mother and *New York Woman* reportedly told Schwartz, "It may be true what you're saying, but we just can't discuss these things in print."[5]

This "no-bad-news" mindset may partially explain the attitude we have seen in the previous chapters, where, in the surprisingly candid words of journalist Sherri Eisenberg, reporters have tried to beautify research on day care with "a great big smiley face of a lead" and have "buried" negative findings "if they mentioned them at all."[6] But another key factor is that the writers, editors and broadcast journalists who cover these issues are often themselves working mothers dependent on day care. Feminist proponents of day care receive the cooperation of a pliant media because, in many cases, they *are* the media. Perhaps because it is so sensitive and personal a topic, it goes virtually unremarked that the great bulk of the stories on day care in the major papers, in the women's magazines and on television are written by working women, many of whom have made out-of-home arrangements for their own children (and who are often reporting on studies carried out by their academic colleagues and counterparts). It is simply unreasonable to expect objective reportage about an issue in which so many of them are deeply invested. This conflict of interest would be immediately apparent if, say, all the reporting on smoking were conducted exclusively by smokers. But with regard to the coverage of day care, no one—not even the editors who assign stories—seems willing to acknowledge the fact that working moms might be less than ideal candidates for the day care beat.

The need for more corporate and government support for institutional day care programs is a more or less unquestioned tenet of those covering the issue. It is assumed to be a "family-friendly" stance, despite the fact that most families would prefer to balance work and home in a way that would allow them to be more engaged with the raising of their children, not less. But the day care solution makes a lot of sense to journalists with children who write about day care. When reporting on findings about the effects of institutional day care by the National Institute of Child Health and Human Development, for instance, Sue Shellenbarger, who writes the "Work & Family" column for the *Wall Street Journal* and who has had extensive experience with day care for her own children, bent over backwards to put them in a day care–friendly light—even if it meant obscuring them in a forest of qualification. "Kids in *high-quality* child care settings, *as gauged by care-giver sensitivity, responsiveness and conversations,* did better *than all other children,* even those in their mother's care, *on cognitive and language tests*" (my italics).[7]

Other cases are more egregious. Susan Chira, now a deputy foreign editor at the *New York Times,* reported on child care issues for the venerable paper while her own children were in day care. During this period, she also wrote a book celebrating day care with the title *A Mother's Place: Choosing Work and Family without Guilt or Blame.*[8] (Imagine a reporter assigned to cover a similarly contentious issue, say, the debate over tobacco, penning a book titled *Smoking without Guilt or Blame.*) The *Times'* own reviewer wrote of the book that "Working mothers could not ask for a better champion."[9]

So determined are reporters covering the child care beat to publicize research favorable to the institutional day care regime that they often fail to point out that the studies they write about have been conducted by professional advocates of that regime. The news articles that greeted the publication of Ellen Galinsky's *Ask the Children: What America's Children Really Think about Working Parents* show how this works. The book's "findings"—that children of working couples are less concerned about the time their parents spend with them than about their work-related stress—were reported as if Galinsky were a disinterested researcher rather than a day care advocate. The *Washington Post's* front-page story reported that Galinsky's "random surveys" found that "contrary to parents' beliefs, most youngsters didn't say they want more time with their parents" but "better communication and more 'focused' time." The *Post* story identified the study's author simply as "researcher Ellen Galinsky, president of the Families and Work Institute, a New York think tank that tracks workplace trends."[10]

None of the stories mentioned that Galinsky has been in the business of promoting day care for the last quarter-century, with ties to the day care industry that date back to the mid-1970s. Before founding the Families and Work Institute, she served for twenty-five years on the faculty of Bank Street College, a training ground for day care workers and pro–day care activism. She has been churning out pro–working mom and pro–day care literature continuously since then, with support from interested corporate and day care industry donors.

Galinsky's 1977 book, *The New Extended Family: Day Care That Works,* written when center-based care was a relatively radical concept for most parents, was termed a "celebration of child care" in the author's acknowledgments, and dedicated in part to the Bank Street Day Care Consultation Group. Here Galinsky sought to dispel the "myth" that parents "are the sole guardians, the protectors, the providers for their children" and to reassure worried parents that the "new extended family" of the day care center is a place where they will find wonderful, dedicated, caring experts who can aid their children's development and share the burden of parenting. The following passage gives a flavor of Galinsky's portrait of center-based care:

> A sentence we heard over and over in the programs we visited was "We want to be an extended family for the parents."
> This might have seemed trite to us had we not seen so many real, vibrant demonstrations of it. All the programs we visited in institutional settings had a home-like ingredient

somewhere in their composition. The Learning Center had a man and a woman at the head of each group, and children clustered in a mixed-age pattern resembling a family.[11]

The book is also an extended argument for greater public support for the then-nascent day care system. "The tenuous position of many centers," wrote Galinsky and her co-author, William Hooks, "is a sad comment on the present position of child care within our culture." According to one day care director quoted in the book, the lamentable fact that "child care help is not yet accepted as a social responsibility" and that society doesn't "demand tax-supported child care" is possible only because "children don't vote." Among other initiatives proposed by Galinsky and Hooks are a system of day care centers "available to anyone who wants [center-based care]" funded by "parents, community, private agencies, and state and local government with appropriate assistance from the federal government," and federal laws mandating the development of "kith and kin systems" in local communities. Another day care director is approvingly quoted envisioning the ideal day care center that such a system might bring into being:

> I would love to see us operate as a community center in the best sense of the word.... A place where supper is served ... and families could have dinner here together. We have a sewing machine—families could sew here. We could have a library. We could buy one book that could be read by five people, and one newspaper that could be read by ten.

This kind of advocacy journalism masked as "research" is a major reason for the one-sidedness of the public debate on day care.

ANOTHER PART OF THE PROBLEM is the conflicting interests, and sometimes the timidity, of child care professionals, as Michael Meyerhoff of the Center for Parent Education has pointed out:

> Over 90 percent of the professionals we deal with agree with our basic position—that full-time substitute care for children under age three is not ordinarily in the best interests of the child. But many of these professionals are involved in situations where it's economically or politically unrealistic to maintain that position. Because of the strong attacks they'd be likely to get, many people are not saying anything.

One poll of pediatricians in the United States showed that 77 percent believe infants six months or younger ought to be cared for at home; another survey by the American Academy of Pediatrics showed a substantial majority of baby doctors consider full-time day care harmful for children under four years of age.[12] Eleanor Galenson, a child psychiatrist in New York, says the same for the psychiatric community. According to Galenson, it is undeniable that "putting infants into full-time daycare is a dangerous practice [but] psychiatrists have been afraid to come out and tell the public this [even though] many of us certainly believe it to be true."[13] Dr. Stanley Greenspan writes similarly that "some of my colleagues have told me they are reluctant to publicly voice their concerns about child care because they fear they will be seen as advocating the return of mothers to full-time home duty."[14]

In the case of the day care research community in the academies, there is clearly more of an ideological component at work. Concerning attempts to deconstruct evidence that unambiguously confirms the irreplaceable nature of the individual care a mother provides, child development expert Penelope Leach forthrightly asserts that "there is a cover-up going on."[15] Leach's blunt assessment is echoed by several insiders who have withstood pressure from their colleagues to refrain from discussing day care risks. Professor Jay Belsky, who has been the lightning rod for the wrath of feminist researchers for years, has expressed dismay at the number of colleagues who have urged him not to publish work that points out the detrimental effects on children of extended periods in group care. "There are a lot of people out there who don't open their mouths [about day care risks]," he says, "because they know how vehement the reaction can be."[16] Several times when Belsky was able to get research about day care risks published in sociological journals (only because of his reputation as a top researcher in the field), those journals departed from their usual format by publishing four negative critiques in rebuttal, accusing him of selective use of data, misrepresentation of findings and personal bias against women. In his rejoinder, Belsky wrote,

> The playing field is by no means even when it comes to considering the strengths and weaknesses of research on a topic as politically and ideologically charged as day care and maternal employment. Some findings, and the methods and analyses that discern them, are simply more "politically correct" than others. For science this is a major problem.[17]

Dr. Mohammadreza Hojat, research associate professor of psychiatry and human behavior at Jefferson Medical College in Philadelphia, is another researcher in child development who has raised the issue of the censorship and "the conspiracy of silence [which] prevails among scientists on the importance of motherhood and the family." According to Hojat, "a new cultural mentality of political correctness" prevailing in academia—and enforced by "interest groups, including extreme feminists or those who personally prefer a nontraditional lifestyle"—makes it all but impossible to discuss the adverse effects of nonmaternal child care. He further complains that prominent academics have even suggested that "research on detrimental effects of nonmaternal care must be interrupted or abandoned."[18] Why do researchers downplay or ignore the evidence pointing to the vital importance of the mother-child bond? Hojat believes that the reasons include "political considerations, personal agendas, and selfish individual interests." The research community is populated by "advocates of nonmaternal care" who are "blindly influenced by empty feminist rhetoric" and "incorrectly believe that infants and toddlers are highly resilient and that the type of early care, maternal or nonmaternal, does not make any difference."

Hojat asserts that ideological considerations are undermining the whole enterprise of child development research. "The cause of science cannot be served if investigators violate basic scientific principles," he explains. "*Objectivity* is one of them. . . . Many investigators on university campuses are themselves in two-career households." Such personal considerations, including the use of day care by the very researchers responsible for objectively investigating its effects, mean that a large number are biased—particularly those "who are mothers themselves, with a need to rationalize their own child-abandonment." This explains the common resort to highly unscientific arguments to deny the importance of findings that indicate serious day care risks, such as contending "that maternal love is a myth created by religious authorities, that motherhood was transformed into a nurturing role by misguided experts in order to keep women imprisoned at home, and that the findings on risk factors associated with early nonmaternal care are the investigator's fantasies."[19]

The bias even reaches the level of overt censorship, Hojat contends. The "dirty secret of editorial bias and scientific censorship" has led to professional journals using "a political rather than a scientific criterion in accepting or rejecting a study or an opinion for publication." Hojat's own experience clearly bears this out. In 1989 he submitted a commentary on an article about working mothers and the need for day care by prominent child development researcher Sandra Scarr and several of her colleagues in the *American Psychologist.* Initially, he received a letter from an associate editor saying that his commentary looked good and that a final decision would be made in two or three months, after the article was sent to consulting editors for the normal review process. Shortly afterward, the editor wrote to say that he had read the commentary with interest but "space demands" prevented him from publishing it. Hojat offered to cut the commentary to one typed page if space was the only consideration. He was told that he would be informed if this was acceptable, but he was never contacted again. (His commentary, along with a sarcastic and abusive rejoinder by Scarr, was eventually published in another academic journal, whose editor agreed that censorship had indeed been the reason for the piece's initial rejection.)

A year later, Dr. Louise Silverstein published a highly provocative article in the *American Psychologist* demanding that "psychologists must refuse to undertake any more research that looks for the negative consequences of other-than-mother care."[20] In language that seemed better suited to *Ms.* magazine than a journal of scientific research, Silverstein justified her call for an "interruption" of research into risk factors related to nonmaternal care by arguing that since "two decades of exhaustive research ... has failed to document consistent, meaningful negative findings," researchers should instead put their energy into documenting "the negative consequences of not providing high-quality, affordable day care."

Aside from the risible notion that research has turned up no meaningful evidence of risks associated with nonmaternal care, Silverstein's paper was loaded with inflammatory feminist rhetoric. Motherhood is portrayed as an "idealized myth" created when "men in politics and the clergy began to glorify motherhood in an attempt to encourage white, middle class women to have more children." Deriding experts such as Spock and Brazelton for needlessly transforming motherhood into a nurturing job, Silverstein attacks fathers in general as "cads" who, because of their desire for "sexual access to many mates," are inclined to deny "responsibility for provisioning any offspring." The mandate of psychology, she suggests, is to take up "the challenge of transforming cads into dads."[21]

Once again, Hojat submitted a commentary to *American Psychologist.* In it he suggested that Silverstein's proposal to abandon research was "against the traditional principle of science," citing the large body of research showing the singular importance of maternal nurturing in healthy child development. He also criticized Silverstein for inviting "further division of the already frail discipline of psychology into a battlefield in which the accumulated knowledge [of child development] will be disgraced" for not being sufficiently feminist. After almost a year of waiting for some response to his submission Hojat inquired about its status, only to receive a curt rejection.[22]

IN THE WAKE OF THE RECENT CONTROVERSIES over the link between day care and aggressiveness, researchers all but admitted to a double standard in dealing with findings that indicate risks from day care. "There's more caution in drawing implications that might be worrisome to parents," said NICHD investigator Robert Pianta. And Allison Clarke-Stewart, a key player in the day care research community for years, conceded that "when you come out with a finding that is negative and scary, you want to make sure you've done every possible analysis."[23] As one of the most public critics of Jay Belsky's research for his reliance on measurements of childhood attachment that are supposedly

antiquated and unsuited to day care children, Clarke-Stewart neglected to mention that she had used these same measurements herself a decade earlier to show that day care had
no ill effects. Belsky was stunned that she had "the intellectual audacity again and again to make the argument that
these avoidant kids in day care are falsely appraised."[24] She
also had the audacity to dedicate her scholarly book on day
care to her son, who "spent his first year in day care so that
this book could be written."[25]

The distortion of methodology to achieve ideologically
palatable results is not unique to research involving day care;
it has become the norm for all the social sciences touching
on family structure. David Blankenhorn of the Institute for
American Values has observed that in order to "deny or minimize the effects of family structure on child well being, sociological researchers regularly twist themselves into
categorical/definitional knots." A recent example: in determining "risk factors" that can undermine the social and emotional development of preschoolers in the United States, a
group of researchers commissioned by the private founda-
tions and government agencies concerned with child development came up with a system to evaluate the relative weight
of the different factors. As part of the rating system they
devised, risk factors related to family structure were simply
defined as "fixed markers," or factors that are not a reasonable basis for public policy recommendations because they
are not subject to change. Blankenhorn remarks that these
types of "almost comically tautological 'findings'" are par
for the course in sociology that deals with questions related
to the family.[26]

In the social sciences there is enormous pressure to down-
grade findings that reflect poorly on the new family structures
endorsed by feminism, such as dual-career families with children in day care. This is reflected in the work of Dr. Sandra
Scarr, now professor emeritus of psychology at the University

of Virginia and a highly influential figure in the day care research community. Since the early 1970s, Scarr has published over two hundred articles and four books related to day care and child development, and her impact on how others approach research in these fields is inestimable. She has been on the faculty of the University of Virginia, the University of Pennsylvania and Yale University, and has served as editor of *Developmental Psychology* and *American Psychologist,* two of the top psychology journals. She has been president of the Society for Research in Child Development, the Behavior Genetics Association and the American Psychological Society.

Scarr has also been a relentless propagandizer for day care. Her 1984 book *Mother Care/Other Care* set out to debunk the notion that the bond between mother and child is of unique importance and that disrupting that bond will cause a child grave harm. Among her contentions in the book are: that a baby has no particular need for its biological mother; that the best thing for an infant is to develop relationships with numerous caregivers; that fathers are no less equipped than mothers to satisfy the needs of an infant; and that it is not necessarily natural for mothers to feel pleasure in fulfilling the needs of their child.[27] Much of the book argues that mothers are simply culturally conditioned to believe that their nurturing is vital for their child. "Why should working mothers feel guilty or deprived?" asks Scarr. "Should they 'suffer' from being away part-time from maternal responsibilities, if they also have paying jobs that are important to them and to the rest of the family? Why the guilt trip?"[28]

Indeed, the emphasis in much of Scarr's writing on the subject has been on the needs of working women rather than the needs of children. "Workplaces afford women (and men) adult companionship, rewards for good work, some financial independence, and a paycheck that says they are real adults in this society," Scarr wrote in one commentary. "As long as their children are not seriously and permanently harmed, women have choices about how to allocate their efforts at home and in the larger society." Public support of day care, in Scarr's view, is the only option for those who support the equality of women. "Those who believe that women should have the same rights as men support quality child care to enable women to be employed, if they so desire. . . . If mothers did not work their family economies and the national economy would collapse." In fact, says Scarr, opposition to public funding of commercial child care can be explained only in terms of the oppression of women: "Keeping government out of child care support and regulation is a subterfuge for opposition to women in the labor force and child care provisions that might allow more mothers to work more comfortably." She feels that exclusive mother-care of infants is a thing of the past, and good riddance. "However desirable or undesirable the ideal of full-time maternal care may be, it is completely unrealistic in the world of the late 20th century."[29]

In reaction to the research compiled by Jay Belsky and others later in the decade indicating that separation of infants and toddlers from their mothers does indeed have detrimental effects on child development, Sandra Scarr and her colleagues responded in baldly political terms, accusing Belsky of having a hidden antifeminist agenda. At one academic conference on child development, she said heatedly to Belsky, "We don't have to talk anymore, you just have to figure out why you're so angry. Why are you so angry, Jay? What are you so angry about all of this?"[30] Scarr accused Belsky of having a personal axe to grind against day care; if he didn't, she argued, he would have emphasized the need for improving center-based care rather than "how can we make mothers feel guilty and stay at home."[31] She dismissed his findings indicating detrimental effects from day care as "backlash against the women's movement" and said they were motivated by an attempt to reverse the professional gains of women. "The advice for women has always been to get out of the workforce," Scarr said. "This is just another way of saying the same thing."

Scarr herself tried to refute Belsky indirectly by redefining aberrant behavior and also maintaining that evolutionary biology made infants relatively immune to poor caregiving environments. Social and intellectual development, Scarr asserted, occurs in infants as a result of biological design, with maternal interaction being more or less irrelevant. If parents feel compelled to take "a few months" off to be with their children, it would make far more sense for them to do it later, when they are toddlers and have a degree of awareness, than when they are infants. Before that, she confidently told the *New York Times* in 1987, "their brains are Jell-O and their memories akin to those of decorticate rodents."[32] Recently, Scarr was asked whether the accumulation of research indicating numerous risk factors related to nonmaternal care had caused her to reconsider. "It's a stupid question," she replied. "Children can thrive under a variety of regimes. What's the big deal?"[33]

Well, part of the big deal is that while using her academic credentials as a platform, Scarr has had a continuing close involvement with day care "regimes." Since 1990, she has served on the board of directors of KinderCare Inc., the largest day care chain in the United States; in 1994 she was elected chairman of the board. Only when she was made chief executive officer of KinderCare in 1995 did she finally leave the faculty of the University of Virginia. Even then, she continued to publish articles in academic journals, and while CEO of KinderCare she also served as president of the American Psychological Society in 1996–1997.

An article that Scarr published in the *Brown University Child and Adolescent Behavior Letter* in 1997 blatantly promotes the industry she was a part of. Arguing against the idea that early formative experience is particularly important for the normal emotional and intellectual development of infants, Scarr writes, "If our species had evolved to require scarce or unusual experiences for normal development to occur, humans would be extinct." Concerning the effort to get parents to devote more time and attention to infants, she asks, "Why evoke worry and guilt in working parents about their children's development when we know that caring parents who engage in culturally ordinary interactions with their children will do just fine?" Unbelievably, she claims that the National Institute of Child Health and Human Development findings up to that point have shown that "the quality of infant care . . . had no impact on young children's development" but that "good quality day care can to some extent make up for poor parenting." Although it is a "theoretical and emotional blow to some experts," she writes, it has become clear "that day care is just as beneficial to children as full-time parental care. . . . We can no longer say that children need full-time maternal care when studies show that other arrangements work just as well to promote healthy development." Society should "re-examine the ideal that children should be so exclusively attached to their mothers that they suffer when their mothers are absent." In closing, she offers a portrait of the "new century's ideal children" that looks suspiciously like an idealized portrait of a day care graduate. These ideal children

> will need shared care to develop essential social and emotional skills to deal with frequent job changes and relocations. They will need to be more sociable and secure with large numbers of new people than were children of the past. Teamwork will be stressed from an early age. Multiple attachments to others will become the ideal. Shyness and exclusive maternal attachment will be seen as dysfunctional. New treatments will be developed for children with exclusive maternal attachments (EMA Syndrome) and those with low sociability scores.

Experts will even claim that "being isolated at home with one adult and no peers" is harmful "and should not be permitted."[34]

None of Scarr's professional colleagues—with the exception of Belsky—has ever challenged her double role as objective researcher and corporate executive.

SANDRA SCARR AND OTHER PROMOTERS of commercial day care emphasize the dependence of both the business community and the nation's economy on the labor of working mothers with young children. It is true that American corporations have worked assiduously in the past quarter-century to draw more married women into the workforce and used institutionalized child care as part of their strategy.

A 1957 conference on "Work in the Lives of Married Women" brought together U.S. economists, business leaders and government representatives to discuss the question of how to utilize the labor (at that time still largely potential) of married women. James P. Mitchell of the Labor Department told the conference that he believed the United States could not "continue to advance our standard of living without the integration of women in greater numbers into the work force." Because manpower needs would become more pressing in the coming years, said Mitchell, the "farsighted employer" will "have to employ women in ever-increasing numbers and in an increasing variety of jobs." Corporate executives in the United States followed this lead when a Commission on the Status of Women called by President Kennedy characterized the more efficient and effective use of women's labor as "a necessity."[35] Thus, business interests were already anticipating "new feminists" like Betty Friedan in their endorsement of the working-mother family model as an economic, if not philosophical, imperative.

Mitchell, we can now see, underestimated the possibilities of capitalizing on the potential workforce of married women of childbearing age; he said that during these years, "the employer is certain to find himself running a poor second to biology."[36] But he proved remarkably prescient in predicting the direction that future employment practices would take. His error was in failing to anticipate the lengths to which employers would go to entice and retain mothers of young children in the workforce.

In a lengthy article several years ago, the *Economist* magazine summarized some of the advantages employers gain from an expanded pool of labor that includes working mothers. One advantage is the new markets created when formerly nonmonetary functions of the family are commercialized: "Being able to draw on a larger pool of available workers improves the quality of labor, reduces the risk of shortages and raises demand, not least for goods and services that will make a working woman's life easier: labor-saving devices, convenience foods, meals out, child care."

As David Blankenhorn of the Institute for American Values has pointed out, from a "child's eye view," many so-called "family-friendly" policies instituted by corporations in the last twenty years are not so much family-friendly as they are corporate-friendly, clearly working to the advantage of companies that wish to retain, or attract, married mothers. Corporate executives admit as much. In 1989, when former British prime minister Margaret Thatcher encouraged mothers to stay home with their young children (which she regarded as an important element in the effort to reduce violent and antisocial behavior by British youth), corporate leaders argued that a scarcity of women in the labor market would push up wages, and British companies responded by offering more liberal maternity leave with guaranteed reemployment. Some companies even introduced new incentives that would wean mothers from their babies and get them back to work faster, such as 25 percent pay raises for the six months after maternity leave.[37] Many companies in the United States offer similar perks. From the perspective of children's well-being, this is anything but a pro-family policy. As Penelope Leach has written, "using financial or career penalties to blackmail women into leaving infants who are scarcely settled into life outside wombs that are still bleeding is no less than barbarous."[38]

Less barbarous, perhaps, but just as motivated by bottom-line considerations are other "family-friendly" policies found among top U.S. corporations. Johnson & Johnson has determined that it is saving four dollars from lower retraining costs and higher productivity for every dollar spent on their Life Works maternity leave and child care program. The chairman and chief executive of Eli Lilly, Randall Tobias, has said that he does not consider his company's expanded family leave and child care programs to be employee benefits so much as tools that "will help us attract, motivate, and retain people who are more likely to be dedicated, more focused, more innovative, and more productive." These "family-friendly" policies have the added advantage of giving larger companies a competitive edge over their smaller competitors, who are often unable to afford such benefits—or tools.

All this helps to explain why corporations have made such a big investment in day care in recent years. Over ten thousand companies in the United States now offer on-site day care, up from fewer than two hundred in 1980.[39] Even more companies have made dependent-care assistance plans available to their employees as part of the benefits package; almost half offer a day care resource and referral service. Companies compete to get onto *Working Mother*'s annual list of "100 Best Companies for Working Mothers." Corporate investment in day care has actually created a network of subsidiary for-profit companies worth more than $100 million. Reportedly, businesses have invested another $200 million in commercial child care through the American Business Collaboration for Quality Dependent Care.

Executives of large corporations are blunt about their motivations in making such investments. Roger Brown, CEO of Bright Horizons, notes that "Companies are investing in child care in a way that is tied to business strategy and not just new benefits."[40] Patagonia, an outdoor-clothing company in California, offers its mothers a fully accredited on-site kindergarten, "lactation-support" services (meaning mothers are allowed to bring their babies into meetings for breastfeeding) and after-school care for older children—all justified by management as a cost-effective means of reducing turnover and absenteeism. Almost three hundred American employers, including Aetna, Eastman Kodak, Cigna and Home Depot, now offer "pumping rooms" where mothers can take regular breaks to attach electric pumps to their breasts to collect the milk in bottles for their infants in day care. Some companies have hired "lactation consultants" to help mothers solve breastfeeding problems. Aetna, one such company, estimates that it saves $1,435 and three days of sick leave per mother of a breast-fed baby—a three-to-one return on their investment.[41] If a company offers on-site care as part of its benefits package, making alternate arrangements may in effect require a working parent to find another job.

The mentality behind the corporate support of the day care regime was captured at a 1996 conference sponsored by the Families and Work Institute. Remarking on the success of his company's day care program, Christian Kjeldsen of Johnson & Johnson acknowledged that it was not a response to employee demand, but was inspired by several articles in business magazines on the changing demographics of the job market. Benefits such as day care would remain a permanent fixture, said Kjeldsen, despite recent downsizing and "early-outs" at the company. In other words, Johnson & Johnson has judged it more cost-effective to warehouse the babies of some employees than to retain the jobs of others whose incomes may be sufficient for their families to avoid recourse to day care. Family-friendly benefits do not, as it turns out, include job security or paying one parent enough to support a family on a single income.[42]

Despite the fact that surveys of working mothers show an overwhelming preference for policies that allow employees to fulfill family responsibilities at home—such as flex-time, part-time, telecommuting or even child tax credits that would allow them to care for their children full-time—the nation's big businesses continue to opt for "work/family" policies that will assure them better control over their workers. This is why over twenty corporate giants—including Aetna, Allstate, American Express, AT&T, Bank of America, Deloitte & Touche, Hewlett Packard, IBM, Johnson & Johnson, Price Waterhouse, ExxonMobil, Texas Instruments, Xerox and Citibank—decided to form the American Business Collaboration for Quality Dependent Care in 1992. Now funded to the tune of $136 million a year, the network bankrolls "school-age, child care, and elder care projects in communities across the country."[43]

Working with corporate interests in formulating these corporate-friendly day care policies are organizations such as Ellen Galinsky's Families and Work Institute. Galinsky provided empirical support for the American Business Collaboration's heavy investment in day care, saying, "Our studies clearly demonstrate that for every dollar companies spend on work-life programs, they get back a return in terms of retention, reduced stress, and greater loyalty."[44] As it happens, the Families and Work Institute receives major funding from many of these same companies, and has carried out studies with grants from big corporate donors. Galinsky also served in an advisory capacity for the U.S. Department of the Treasury's report *Investing in Child Care* in 1998, which emphasized the same business-friendly investment in day care.

It comes as no surprise, therefore, that such corporate- and government-sponsored studies as *Investing in Child Care* invariably recommend greater "subsidization of quality out-of-home care while suggesting little or nothing to promote parental care," in the words of Harvard's Richard Gill.[45] Similarly, new government regulations requiring businesses to provide family leave and tax breaks given to corporations for establishing day care support for employees converge with the interests of the bigger corporations, who often see such measures as yet another way of gaining a competitive advantage. Large businesses can easily absorb the costs—and retain the services of married-mother workers while they're at it—while smaller competitors founder under the regulatory burden. The federal government, too, has a direct interest in subsidizing the day care regime by mandating "family-friendly" benefits. Maximizing the number of married mothers in the work force also means maximizing Social Security payments and income tax revenues.

Indeed, government officials now speak of day care in terms of economic competitiveness and national security. In the midst of the stock market boom of the late 1990s, Secretary of the Treasury Robert Rubin worried that "this prosperity will mask the challenges that we face. A key question is: how do we create an environment that will increase productivity? The answer is that we need a flexible and mobile workforce to which everyone can contribute to the limits of their ability." This workforce, he argued, needs federally subsidized day care.[46]

THE LAST AND MOST IMPORTANT ELEMENT of the national coalition working for the establishment of day care as a social norm is the $36 billion commercial day care industry itself and its lobbyists in Washington, D.C. Some elements of this lobby consist of "fellow travelers"—those promoting day care indirectly under the banner of supporting early child education and child well-being, and "early childhood educators" whose institutional associations give them a vested interest in the expansion of day care.[47]

There are also "pro-child" professional associations that have become lobbies for the day care industry as a result of their longtime defense of center-based care. These associations have even welcomed into their ranks the day care entrepreneurs, franchisers and for-profit centers, lending professional status and credibility to representatives of the day care industry as part of a coalition whose primary task is "serving children." This type of legitimization process has been going on for years. At a 1982 conference of the National Association for the Education of Young Children (NAEYC)—an association whose express purpose is "to serve and act on behalf of the needs and rights of young children"—representatives of industry gave workshops with titles like "Yes, Child Care CAN Be Profitable!" and "Regulation of a New Phenomenon—Drop-in Child Care." The latter presentation was made by a representative of "Check-a-Child, Inc."[48] Unsurprisingly, not only for-profit care but casual and "drop-in" care are now associated with the "education" of children.

Center-based chains have even commercialized the care— perhaps "storage" is a better word—of sick children. These enterprises give their sick-child programs comforting names like "Chicken Soup" to disguise what is going on. One advertisement for day care for sick children says that for $30 a day, a sick child will be cared for in one of the following rooms: the "Sniffles Room" for those with respiratory ailments or colds; the "Popsicle Room" for children with diarrhea or vomiting; or the "Polka Dot Room" for those with chickenpox.[49]

Organizations like the NAEYC also put out day care advocacy articles. A 1987 NAEYC article declared:

> The question of whether or not children should be in child care has become obsolete. We have also been able to move

beyond this question because 20 years of research on child care allayed our worst fears that nonmaternal care is inevitably harmful to children. To the contrary, the overwhelming message was that children in good quality child care show no signs of harm and children from low-income families may actually show improved cognitive development.[50]

The studies cited by the authors in a footnote, however, don't even come close to supporting such an unqualified endorsement of day care; in fact they point to considerable risks including increased aggressiveness, social inhibition with adults and negative interactions with other children. Surveying the documentation, one analyst remarked, "how any day-care advocate can read this research, *let alone cite it* as proof" that children in good-quality child care show no signs of harm is "almost beyond comprehension."[51]

Bettye Caldwell, president of NAEYC in the 1980s, regularly denounced reports about bad conditions in day care and described her mission as improving day care's public image. One first-hand report she tried to dismiss was a story about a center where children expectantly looked up and greeted any adult entering the room with cries of "Mommy!" Caldwell said that in all her years of experience with day care centers, she had never seen anything like this. "Either they hid those children when I came by or that's a gross distortion of the reality that's out there," she charged. In response, Deborah Fallows commented,

> Bettye Caldwell may not have seen day care centers like those ... described, but I have, and I did not have to look very hard. There are two possible explanations for the attitude Caldwell expressed: either she is unaware of what day care centers are really like, which is almost impossible to imagine, or she is well aware but finds it harmful for the day care cause to have people dwell on the "negatives."[52]

Because Caldwell and her successors at NAEYC represent not only "early child education" advocates but also day care entrepreneurs and franchisers, this further compromises the notion that they are working in the interests of young children. "There is a popular notion that somehow it is wrong for day care centers to make a profit off of the children they serve," Caldwell argued twenty years ago. "No one objects to authors of children's books, pediatricians, toymakers making profits. . . . To single out day care as an exception makes no sense at all. We should all be able to make a decent living from what we are doing." This sounds less like child advocacy than typical special interest corporate lobbying.

And indeed, the NAEYC and its affiliates engage in the same kind of questionable activity as is typical in lobbying. In one of the only reports on day care lobbying available, the Council on Child Day Care and Early Childhood Programs for the state of Virginia documented the illegal diversion of state child care funds to the Virginia Child Care Resource and Referral Network (a state affiliate of NAEYC). Because of this group's influence, the regulations for three state-sponsored centers were drawn up in such a way that only members of the group qualified for the contracts. The report warned that similar conflicts of interest among day care lobbyists were occurring across the country.[53]

Critics like Deborah Fallows have pointed out that the for-profit day care system necessarily works against "quality" care since profit margins can be maintained only by keeping relatively high ratios of children per caregiver and skimping on funds for local centers in the interests of shareholder profits or executive salaries. The for-profit system also has an inherent interest in just meeting, but not exceeding, minimum standards set by the state, with one study noting that "cost-cutting methods used by the proprietary centers that were owned by chains went beyond efficiency into areas that seriously affected the quality of care."[54] As this statement indicates, these concerns apply especially to chain-operated day care establishments such as KinderCare Inc., which runs more than 1,100 day care centers in thirty-eight states. Kinder-Care was founded in 1969 by a real estate developer named Perry Mendel who recognized the profits to be made from the ever-increasing numbers of working mothers. The story of KinderCare's success in the day care market highlights the contradictions in simultaneously lobbying for a higher quality of care for children and representing for-profit operations. "If the child development experts place prime importance on the question of staff pay," writes Fallows, "so does Kinder-Care, but in the opposite way. KinderCare holds a notoriously hard line on its overall pay policies." While KinderCare and its defenders are quick to assert that the dynamics of for-profit day care are not detrimental to quality, in practice they sacrifice quality at every turn in order to cut costs and increase profits.[55]

Since the 1970s, the whole day care establishment has been highly critical of, even hostile toward, family-based and neighborhood-based care, and has exercised its influence to see that these smaller operators are not given the accredited status that would enable the parents of their wards to qualify for day care–related tax benefits. The implication is that these "unqualified" caregivers present dangers to children, both because they lack regulation (and hence are probably of questionable quality) and because abuse is more likely to occur in such an informal setting. In truth, this is wrong on both counts. A study by the Department of Health and Human Services found that the average ratio of adults to children was far lower among unregulated day care providers (most of them family- or home-based care). The study also noted that over half of the parents with children in these family-based care operations had known the caregiver six months or longer before placing the child there; that one-third of parents have a close personal friendship with the family provider and another third consider the caregiver a casual friend; that over half of the children in these family day care settings live within a few blocks of the caregiver's home; and that three-fourths of parents rate these caregivers as having a "loving" relationship with their children. Family day care poses much less of a health threat to children than does commercial day care—disease transmission is significantly lower.[56] In addition, the most notorious cases of abuse have occurred at fully licensed centers.[57] Thus, according to every reasonable measure of quality, family-based care is superior to center-based care on the criteria of child development experts themselves. Even though parents overwhelmingly prefer informal family- or home-based day care arrangements when they have to rely on someone else, tax credits are available only to those parents who use the regulated, accredited commercial centers.

The day care lobby continually points to the "crisis" of the insufficient supply of "affordable, high-quality" day care for the growing number of working parents who need it. Demand for day care, it is argued, will increase inexorably as married mothers continue to enter the workforce in greater numbers and the proportion of single-parent families grows. Straight-line projections are used to show that the current supply of commercial day care is inadequate to meet future demand and requires increased federal subsidies to remedy the situation. But in fact, there is no real indication of a shortage of supply in commercial day care. Penelope Leach has pointed out that day care advocates use forecasts of increasing demand which "assume that the children of any woman in the labor force will require formal full-time day care, completely ignoring all forms of joint parenting, all informal arrangements, and the range of work options (such as part-time work and flextime) which are preferred by many women wishing to combine working and caring."[58] As it is, the federal government provides more than twice as much assistance through tax exemptions and credits to parents using commercial day care as for those who use family and relative care or those who stay at home with their own children.[59] If there is a shortage, it is a shortage of options for parents who want to avoid putting their children in commercial day care centers.

FIVE

Working Parents' Necessity or Yuppie Subsidy?

The resort to professional day care, it is said, is simply a "fact of modern life," with financial pressures and professional demands conspiring to give working parents no other choice. Rather than argue about irrelevancies like whether young children would be better off at home, we should acknowledge the reality of the reconfigured modern family and invest in improving the quality of commercial day care, not least for the sake of the preschool children who need it. Attempts to turn back the clock to some idyllic era of exclusive maternal care for young children inside the home (an era, we are assured, that never actually existed anyway) are worse than useless, they are positively harmful since they don't acknowledge the real problems of real families today. Only the wealthy can afford the luxury of having one parent stay at home with young children. Failing to make "high-quality, affordable" day care available to any family that needs it is an insidious form of economic and social discrimination, especially against low-income families and single mothers, whose life choices are circumscribed.

This storyline is so prevalent that it forms the unquestioned premise of almost all public discussion of day care. The only problem with it is that it's almost exactly the reverse of the truth.

In reality, the families most likely to use center-based day care are those earning over $75,000 a year. Conversely, the families most likely to rely on friends or relatives to care for their children are on the lower end of the income scale.[1] In fact, the family income bracket with the highest number of stay-at-home moms is those earning $20,000–$24,999, hardly a group living in the lap of luxury.[2] The same pattern holds for the percentages of mothers returning to work before their babies are a year old. In 1998, 69 percent of women with family incomes between $50,000 and $75,000 returned to work within their child's first year (two-thirds of them full-time), while only 49 percent of mothers with family incomes between $10,000 and $20,000 did so.[3]

But do lower-income families perhaps use day care less only because they can't afford it? If day care centers were more fully subsidized, would poorer mothers use them in greater numbers? A survey of low-income mothers completed by University of Connecticut researchers in 1996 found that there was no basis for claiming that "prohibitive expense ... [is] the greatest hindrance to obtaining formal, licensed child care." In fact, respondents were half again more likely to say that "lack of trust" in commercial day care providers, not cost, was the reason they did not put their children in center-based care. The researchers themselves concluded that "it should not be assumed that a family that cannot afford a day care center would prefer a center even if it were made convenient and affordable.... Certainly, services should not be increased if they will not be used even if they are made more affordable."[4]

It is also instructive to look at who is using the currently allowable child care tax credit when considering whether the "child care crisis" is truly a matter of insufficient affordable center-based commercial care for the children of working parents. Remarkably, only 3 percent of the child care tax credit goes to families in the bottom 30 percent of family income (and of course none to families caring for their own children). Families with incomes in the top 30 percent take more than

half of the $2.5 billion to $3 billion that the federal government allots each year. In effect, therefore, the credit for child
care is largely a subsidy used by the relatively wealthy.[5]

The dependent care tax credit is among the most costly
credits in terms of federal revenue. The subsidy for households purchasing commercial day care often exceeds $7,000
per year, and many in Congress are pushing to increase it.
Dual-income families get almost all of these benefits. In the
case of any other "tax break for the wealthy," liberals would
be outraged; but since this particular benefit conforms with
the feminist social vision, liberals love it.[6]

In addition to this special subsidy in the tax code for individuals, tax laws currently allow employers to provide up to
$5,000 in child care benefits tax-free, as well as letting them
provide on-site day care services without counting their value
as taxable income. Another allowed option is to shelter from
taxes the income that employees use to pay for day care.
Aside from blatantly favoring one choice in parenting among
the families of employees, this scheme is plainly anti–free
market in that it undermines the businesses and livelihoods
of private, unsubsidized, family-based day care providers.
Yet Republicans have regularly voted to give businesses such
tax breaks.

Day care subsidies have clearly encouraged many reluctant parents to put their children in commercial facilities.
Larger numbers of parents are doing so than ever before,
while the use of care by relatives has been on the decline.
Many of these parents have decided that putting their young
children in day care facilities is worth the price of separation
because a second income will allow them, down the line, to
provide the kind of material and educational benefits their
children will need to forge their way in the world.

But as columnist and former presidential speechwriter
Peggy Noonan has written, the calculations that parents
make about the advantages their children derive from more

money at the expense of parental time are often in error—
and sometimes unconsciously made in self-justification:

> I see a lot of parents who are straining to get ahead and
> maybe not noticing that they're leaving their kids behind. I
> see mothers scrambling to get to the office, make the money,
> grow the career, rise in the world. But I can see that their chil-
> dren very often don't benefit as much as the parents might
> hope from all this attainment. It's more like the children are
> paying the price for it. . . .
>
> We tell ourselves that we work so hard and have so little
> time for the kids because we need the money. For some of us,
> this is true—single mothers have no choice, nor do wives
> with struggling husbands. But not all of us are working to
> pay the mortgage and the bills. Some of us are working for
> the Porsche or for vacations or for status.[7]

Indeed, when one considers that per capita consumption
has almost tripled since 1960[8] and that the best-educated
mothers with the highest-earning spouses are the group
whose work outside the home has increased at the fastest
rate, it is difficult to gainsay Noonan's implication that the
desire for a higher standard of living is a factor in the decision of many mothers with young children to work outside
the home. But it is probably a less remunerative decision
than they think. It has been calculated that the median after-
tax income of married mothers who work is less than
$20,000; with the costs of commuting, meals, clothing and
other work-related expenses, that second job nets just over
$10,000. Since day care of reasonable quality costs over $9,000
a year per child, it is clear that the decision for mother to
work for the sake of bolstering the family income makes little financial sense for most families—and this is why the
whole scheme can't work without massive subsidies.[9]

But there are other considerations that make the decision
for a couple to forgo that second income during the children's

preschool years seem irrational or difficult to entertain. For one thing, the expense of raising children today is daunting. Some estimates have put the cost of raising one child through the age of seventeen at $250,000; when the lost income of a stay-at-home parent is factored in, the "opportunity cost"—not only in salary, but in lost retirement savings, pensions and other benefits—can easily exceed $1 million. Ironically, a sizeable portion of the soaring cost of childrearing has been in the area of commercial child care: expenses for education and child care have increased from 1 percent to 10 percent of total childrearing costs in the last twenty years.[10]

Such figures are often presented as evidence that the demand for subsidies is coming from people of modest means; but this doesn't seem to be the case. The standard day care advocacy line that only wealthy families can afford the "luxury" of having a stay-at-home parent is completely false. In 1998, traditional families consisting of married couples in which only the husband worked had a median income of $41,883; families in which both parents worked had a median income of $64,026.[11] Among families with preschool children beneath the poverty line, traditional families outnumbered families headed by single mothers.[12] Thus, single-income families making financial sacrifices in order for one parent to stay at home are often subsidizing rich, dual-career yuppies who get tax credits for putting their children in commercial care.

Characterizing the demand for more day care subsidies as a "working women's issue" is not accurate either. Some of the biggest fans of day care are men—specifically, husbands who like the benefit of a second income and who don't have to suffer the guilt of separation that most mothers feel. Polling has consistently shown that support for commercial day care and the subsidies necessary to sustain it is no higher among women than it is among men.

While many relatively well-off, dual-income parents actually want to put their children in commercial day care, in the vast majority of families the only reason one parent does not stay home with the children is financial pressure. With all the talk of rising family incomes and standards of living, this is easy to lose sight of. But as the tax burden on families with children has risen dramatically over the past quarter-century and the cost of living has soared, the average income of men has actually declined. A recent review of economic trends affecting families in the 1990s notes that "for the past two decades, American families in the middle of the income distribution masked men's stagnating wages by reducing the number of children and increasing wives' labor force participation."[13] In other words, median family income hasn't fallen precipitously in the last quarter-century only because wives are working more and earning more than ever before. In recent years, as economist Lester Thurow has pointed out, "the median American female came to the economic rescue of the median American male."[14]

As the single-income family ceases to be the statistical norm, prices for family commodities adjust to dual-income standards. The spreading income gap between families with a parent at home and dual-income families is apparent when one looks at how the market has accommodated the realities of the new domestic economy. Allan Carlson of the Howard Center has shown that between 1970 and 1988 the cost of housing for families where the wife is not in the paid labor force rose by 64 percent relative to income, compared with a 38 percent increase for families with working wives. He maintains that similar "shifts in the terms of trade" to the disadvantage of single-earner families could be plotted for other consumer commodities.[15] Carlson has calculated that as recently as 1976, 40 percent of all jobs still paid enough to support a family of five in minimal comfort; by 1987 only 25 percent of jobs paid such a wage.[16] And in the

1990s the decline in the purchasing power of traditional, single-earner families continued unabated. It is becoming more difficult for the traditional single-income family to afford the normal and necessary expenses of family life. It is hardly an exaggeration to say that dual-income families constitute America's new aristocracy. Whereas in 1969 dual-income families constituted only 41 percent of married-couple families with incomes over $100,000 (adjusted for inflation), by 1995 they were 98 percent of that category.[17]

In light of these factors, there is good reason to take seriously the economic stress that influences families to hold on to that second income—and to question the notion that a large percentage of American families actually prefer to use day care and therefore demand more public support for it.

DESPITE THE MASSIVE GROWTH of dual-career families and the use of institutional day care for young children, there is every indication that the vast majority of parents are not happy with the situation and won't be any happier with more publicly supported day care. Public Agenda, a nonpartisan polling agency based in New York, released a comprehensive survey in 2000 on the subject of how parents, employers and "children's advocates" view the issue of child care. Its findings, little covered at the time, are fascinating. According to the survey, parents prefer one parent staying at home over a "quality" day care center as the best arrangement for children under five by a margin of 70 percent to 6 percent, while 71 percent agree with the statement that "parents should only rely on a day care center when they have no other option." If nonparental care is necessary, 78 percent of the parents surveyed believe that depending on a grandparent or other close relative is the best solution. But 79 percent agree that "no one can do as good a job of raising children as their own parents," while 63 percent hold that it is not possible for even "a top-notch day care center" to provide care as good as what a child would get from a parent at home.

Low-income parents have a markedly more pronounced concern about the adequacy of center-based care than do high-income parents. A full 80 percent of young mothers between the ages of eighteen and twenty-nine with preschool children profess the desire to stay home with them rather than continue to work. By a margin of 81 percent, parents believe that children are "more likely to get the affection and attention they need" with a stay-at-home parent than in a day care center. Explaining the unexpected skepticism about day care reflected in the survey, Public Agenda president Deborah Wadsworth said that the desire of parents "to make sure that their children absorb the values that they believe in is almost tangible."[18]

This aversion to day care is confirmed when we look at the policy options that parents prefer. The survey reported that parents want policies that would "make it easier and more affordable for one parent to stay at home" over those that would "improve the cost and quality of child care" by a margin of 62 percent to 30 percent. Despite the incessant references of day care advocates to a "child care crisis" facing parents in the form of a lack of affordable, high-quality commercial care, 68 percent of the parents surveyed by Public Agenda responded that child care is "not much of a problem" for them. Summarizing the findings, the study's authors wrote that

> by overwhelming margins, parents say the love and sustained attention a parent offers simply cannot be replicated by other forms of care. Parents also believe that children raised by a stay-at-home parent are more likely to learn strong values and considerate behavior than children in child care. When a parent cannot be home, parents say, child care by a close relative is best.[19]

The polarization over day care is quite obvious when we compare the opinions of child development "experts" with those of parents. In most respects, the views and priorities of the two groups stand in direct contradiction. Among the experts, 78 percent think the attention that children get in high-quality day care is just as good as what they would get from a parent at home (compared with only 34 percent of parents). Only 13 percent of the children's advocates surveyed thought that "too few families choosing to keep one parent at home with children at least during the first few years" was a very serious problem, but 86 percent of this same group felt that the "lack of affordable, quality day care centers" was of grave importance—the opposite of parents' views. While 68 percent of advocates thought that the best government child care policy would be to "move toward a universal, national child care system," just 6 percent supported providing "tax breaks that encourage families to have one parent stay at home." When considering the enormous disparity between the views of parents and those of the "children's advocates," the Public Agenda study's authors tentatively suggest that perhaps "advocates have not successfully transmitted [their] vision to the vast majority of America's parents" and that they "may also have underestimated the strength of most parents' competing vision."[20]

To put it more candidly, the opinions expressed by parents in the survey represent a dramatic failure of the day care establishment to convince them that the brave new world of dual-career families with children cared for by professionals is a desirable thing. And despite all the rhetoric to the contrary, parents are clearly not clamoring for more public support of center-based care.

The Public Agenda survey confirms a large body of polling that the media and the day care lobby have done their best to ignore.[21] A nationwide survey published by *Parents* magazine and the I Am Your Child Foundation in May of 2000 showed an astounding 77 percent of mothers responding that they would stay home full-time to raise their children if they could, a figure that was remarkably consistent with numerous other polls along the same lines in the past decade. Significant majorities of both fathers and mothers were unhappy with the limited amount of time they were able to spend with their children. More than three times as many parents in this poll preferred informal care arrangements to a formal child care center.[22] Illogically, the I Am Your Child founder and day care advocate Rob Reiner released a statement implying that the survey confirmed the necessity of the day care lobby's agenda: "What this poll clearly indicates is that we need to provide a comprehensive support system—access to health care, increased quality child care, expanded family leave, and government and business support—so that parents and caregivers can provide children with a good, healthy start in life."[23]

The *Parents*/I Am Your Child survey results track very closely with other recent polling data. A detailed *Los Angeles Times* survey from June 2001 showed 68 percent of California fathers and 69 percent of mothers agreeing that "it is much better for the family if the father works outside the home and the mother tends to the children." In fact, a majority of *working* mothers (59 percent) felt the same way. As far as personal choices go, this poll showed that 50 percent of all fathers and 81 percent of mothers said they would rather stay home with their children than work outside the home if circumstances allowed. Well over half of working mothers felt guilty about leaving their children in day care. Two-thirds said that leaving children with a relative would be preferable to putting them in center-based care. This poll too showed extremely low levels of support for subsidizing commercial day care: 28 percent said it was a good idea, while 80 percent supported tax breaks for families where one parent stays home with children under age five.

Once more, the child development "experts" were in denial about the poll's meaning. Most disregarded it completely; one of the few children's advocates quoted could barely conceal her disdain for the culturally retrograde views of parents. "It may be wishful—or wistful—thinking," said Sandi Schwarm, executive director of the USC child care programs. "Even Ozzie and Harriet and all the 1960s and 1950s serials— that wasn't the way families really were. That was the ideal. The house was always clean."[24] Another expert, Marcy White-book, described as a children's advocate in Berkeley, Califor-nia, was exasperated that parents didn't seem to understand what is in their best interests. "The bad news" she said, "is that because we don't have a good child care system and because we leave people to fend for themselves about these issues, women aren't asking for help that they really deserve and that could make their lives and their children's lives better."[25]

GIVEN THEIR PREFERENCE FOR TAKING care of their own chil-dren at home, how do we account for the fact that by the early 1990s, just 27 percent of working mothers quit their jobs around the time they gave birth, and 52 percent returned to work after six months?[26] Why, according to the figures published in one study, do 75 percent of working mothers with children work full-time if only 15 percent of them pre-fer to do so?[27] Unless they are willing to dismiss all the sur-vey responses as hypocritical, policymakers would do well to acknowledge that one of the primary factors is financial pressure. There is no doubt a large element of cultural pres-sure as well: young women who have been told all their lives by the popular culture and the media that the pursuit of a glamorous career is more important than having a family are not likely to let go of that vision very easily. Most work-ing mothers are deeply conflicted—hence the prevalence of the word "guilt" in the debate over day care. According to one study, a majority of young mothers are "distressed" over the clash between "their belief in the exclusivity of the mothering role" and their professional lives.[28]

But there are some indications in recent years that the experience of unfulfilling dead-end jobs does more to convince young mothers of the relative attractions of home and family, even in a culture that tends to portray motherhood as an unfortunate and inconvenient interruption of personal and professional fulfillment. They have discovered what G. K. Chesterton pointed out at the beginning of the last century: that the feminist romanticizing of the workplace has more basis in ideology than in fact. "These people seem to think that the ordinary man is a Cabinet Minister," he wrote.

> They are always talking about man going forth to wield power, to carve his own way, to stamp his individuality on the world, to command and to be obeyed.... Indeed, he is not so free. Of the two sexes the woman is in the more powerful position. For the average woman is at the head of something with which she can do as she likes; the average man has to obey orders and do nothing else. He has to put one dull brick on another dull brick, and do nothing else; he has to add one dull figure to another dull figure, and do nothing else.[29]

Economist and author Jennifer Roback Morse writes in a similar vein today: True, the postindustrial office is characterized by considerably more mobility and more autonomy than the mechanical and regimented drudgery that Chesterton described. But Morse argues that despite the attractions and perks of the modern workplace, the reality that the majority of working mothers find there is far from the romantic picture painted by feminist advocates of "having it all":

> It is attachment to their wives and children that keeps men reporting as truck mechanics and cab drivers. It is a sense of

loving duty that keeps men standing on subway platforms
that lead to fluorescent-lit offices. The drudgery of caring for
small children is nothing compared to the drudgery of fac-
tory work or a data entry job. For many workers, the tedium
of a humdrum job is relieved more than anything else by
coming home to a noisy household. . . . Instead of introduc-
ing their own children to great literature and world history,
bright women are sequestered in university offices, grading
piles of illegible midterms written by other people's children.
How did we forget that guiding our offspring requires knowledge far more subtle, and pays bounties far richer, than most
jobs?[30]

Many mothers who have been in the workplace are experi-
encing the reality that Morse describes. Recent statistics show
a slight downturn in the percentage of mothers returning to
work during the first year of their child's life, from 59 percent in 1998 to 55 percent in 2000.[31] Several years ago, an
article in *Newsweek* noted that mothers between 36 and 40
were increasingly choosing part-time work after the birth of
a first child, and leaving the workforce altogether with the
birth of a second.[32]

There is little enthusiasm about the day care choice even
among those parents who, for whatever reason, must rely on
nonparental care. Again, the evidence is unambiguous: they
overwhelmingly prefer informal arrangements and try to
avoid commercial day care centers if at all possible. The small
percentage of working parents who actually *are* enthusiastic
for the day care regime, seeing it as a liberation from the burdens of motherhood rather than a necessary evil, are predom-
inantly upper-class, college-educated elites who inhabit the
higher echelons of the corporate world, academia and the
professions. Occasionally, these demographics are acknowledged by day care proponents. "The truth is," feminist critic
Katha Pollitt recently admitted, "the day care debate has
always been about college-educated working moms."[33] For

this small group of day care enthusiasts, the goal of universal, subsidized child care represents an important cultural endorsement of careerism over full-time motherhood. These career-oriented mothers are convinced that in order to compete fully and on an equal footing with men in the job market, they must be relieved of the burden of caring for their children. But this relief, in the form of tax-subsidized and corporate-supported day care, comes at the expense of single-income families, who are already making considerable financial sacrifices for one parent to be with the children. They are the ones paying for such a regime, both through tax subsidies and because of the uneven playing field for single-earner heads of families. The so-called "mommy wars" are not simply the result of overheated rhetoric on both sides of the day care debate; they are a natural consequence of the fact that the increasing push for national day care comes at the expense of mothers at home—and those who would rather be at home.

While day care advocates insist that pursuing a demanding career and being a terrific parent would be perfectly compatible if only government and corporate interests would invest more in quality day care, most working parents today recognize that this ideal is neither possible nor desirable. Their daily reality is closer to that described by a "disillusioned feminist" a decade ago: "The reality of feminism is a lot of frenzied and overworked women dropping kids off at daycare centers. If the child is sick, they just send along some children's Tylenol and then rush off to underpaid jobs that they don't even like."[34]

Penelope Leach has described the inherent emotional tensions that many working mothers unwillingly go through:

> Many parents—especially mothers—live like trapeze artists: always striving to maintain a balance between opposing obligations, always anticipating the trivial slip—chicken pox, an evening conference—that will spell disaster. Most stressful

of all, perhaps, is the perpetual feeling of inadequacy that comes from never having quite enough time or single-mindedness to give to work or home. Whether a woman gives today's priority to children or to work, she may face tomorrow with unresolved feelings of guilt and regret.[35]

This is precisely the reality that day care advocates cannot afford to acknowledge. In truth, mothers who want to put their preschoolers into day care are atypical. But rather than deal with the unpopularity of the day care regime, advocates habitually argue that the increasing reliance on day care shows that parental care is an antiquated ideal. Senator Christopher Dodd, for instance, one of the most relentless proponents of expanding day care subsidies on Capitol Hill, has argued that although mothers caring for their own preschool children may be a desirable social ideal, it is an outdated one.[36] If parental care of young children is portrayed as an antiquated notion, this allows day care advocates to contend that the interests of the day care lobby and those of "working parents" are one and the same.

Occasionally, however, the façade cracks. At a Brookings Institution conference on day care in 1999 (which Senator Dodd participated in), what was intended to be a discussion of strategies to achieve an increase in tax credits for parents who put their children in commercial care turned into an argument over why high-income, dual-earner families should be subsidized by families who sacrifice to keep one parent at home with the children. To the distress of the conference moderator, one questioner innocently asked why "we're providing credits to people with unlimited incomes," characterizing it as "bizarre." The resulting exchange is worth quoting in full.

Conference Participant: Well, it's not so bizarre, because there is a cost of earning income. If you're earning wage income and salary income, it costs money. You have to take care of children and you have to incur other kinds of expenses, and those expenses are just as true for families where the combined income is $500,000 as they are for families where the combined income is $20,000.

Questioner: Yes, but why are taxpayers subsidizing them?

Conference Participant: Taxpayers are not subsidizing them.

Questioner: Sure, they are.

Conference Participant: In what sense? The basic idea of the income tax is that you want to scale the tax liability according to families' ability to pay. Then you try to make to me the case that two families, each with $80,000, one earning it with one wage earner and another potential wage earner staying home caring for children has the same expense of earning that $80,000 as a family where there are two breadwinners, each earning $40,000.

Questioner: That's not the question, though.

Conference Participant: It is the question.

Questioner: No, it's not.

Conference Participant: I understand. There's an equity issue there. But you're talking about relative equity for an $80,000 family and a gross lack of equity for families who have no discretionary income. Your argument—and I don't think it would go over very well with many members of the current Congress, is simply that the income tax system isn't progressive enough. That's your argument. You're saying that tax liabilities for people with low total incomes should be lower relative to people with higher incomes. That's not the argument about children. If children represent an expense that must be borne by families where there's only one potential wage earner and that wage earner's out earning money, and to [other] families with two potential wage earners in which both potential wage earners are earning money, then fairness demands that we more lightly tax the families with two breadwinners than the family with one breadwinner and one stay-at-home parent.

Questioner: You keep bringing up this $80,000 in income earned by one person versus two persons. That's not the issue. The issue is $80,000 earned by two parents versus the family that's earning $40,000 because the other parent has chosen not to go out and get another job and get [the family income] up to that $80,000. That's the argument.

Conference Participant: Your argument is you want a more progressive tax system. That's separate from children. You want to tax the family with $40,000 more lightly than we currently do and a family with $80,000 more heavily. That is not relevant.

Questioner: No, that's not it. And maybe if you'd let me finish what I was saying, you would have heard that. The issue is that some families are choosing to not earn that second income in order to stay home with their kids. Okay? So they are not getting the $80,000 income. They are maybe getting a $50,000 income. Now, if what we're going to do is support families with children, should we, in fact, make some level of tax equity there for the parent who sacrifices? You know, [reward the family] who basically said, all right, I'm not going to have $80,000 in income. We're going to live on $50,000. That is going to be our income. And that's what we're going to live on as opposed to my going back to work and spending $10,000 on child care. . . . How do you get tax equity between those who have chosen to forgo that second income and those who have chosen to go to work and have their children in child care full time and pay $10,000 a year in child care?

Conference Moderator: We're probably not going to resolve this particular debate today. [Laughter.]³⁷

The exchange perfectly captures the mentality of day care advocates, from the conceit that single-earner families are well-off and parents who stay at home to raise their children are "potential earners" who should be penalized, to the fanciful notion that subsidies for parents who put their kids in day care centers are really programs "about children" and spending money in their best interests.

That mentality is also expressed in a disdain for any mothers stupid enough to give up their jobs for the sake of their children. When Massachusetts governor Jane Swift gave birth to twins in office and some suggested that her plan to have them join her two-year-old daughter in day care might indicate some incompatibility between being a great governor and being a marvelous mom, Illinois lieutenant governor Corinne Wood snarled, "I hope by the time [the twins] are grown, the idea that their mother . . . was expected by some to relinquish her job responsibilities . . . will be an antiquated notion that . . . all of society will view with disbelief."[38] According to all the survey data available, it's an "antiquated" notion that most parents view as plain common sense.

SIX

The Family under Siege

The primary social functions of the family are intimately connected with the rearing and socializing of children. The formation of children's intelligence, moral sense, empathy with others and sense of identity have always been regarded as among the most fundamental of parental responsibilities. And the time that parents devote to this task—the extent to which they invest themselves in the process of helping their children to become mature adults with the ability to love others and function in useful and autonomous ways—has traditionally been regarded as the measure of parental devotion. This understanding of parenting, indeed the very function of the family as the first school of social virtues, is challenged by the day care agenda and directly attacked by the ideology that undergirds it.

One might think that in propounding such a revolutionary doctrine—that our traditional notions of the family and the primary formative role of parents are antiquated and unsuited to the realities of modern life—the burden of proof would be on those calling for drastic changes in the established familial order. Yet, as we have seen from the debate over the detrimental effects of day care on children, this has not been the case. The proponents of institutional day care insist on irrefutable proof that institutional, center-based care is truly damaging to children in measurable ways like academic performance and emotional adjustment—and even when proof is provided they insist that "other factors" may be at play. The truth is that their determination to justify the day care regime trumps any evidence. And what they are determined to bring about is the surrender of parental responsibilities.

Many who entered the field of day care work with the best intentions of providing a loving environment conducive to the healthy development of children have become disillusioned upon observing what even the best center-based care does to the parent-child relationship. In *The Day Care Decision,* William and Wendy Dreskin tell the story of their own experience in setting up a high-quality day care center in the San Francisco area. Beginning with teachers who had graduate training, low child-to-adult ratios, the best in educational equipment and an excellent curriculum, the Dreskins opened first a half-day preschool, then a full-day operation when more and more dual-income families asked for it. "We were going to offer a quality program," they later wrote. "We did not have the slightest suspicion that there might be a serious problem with even the best day care programs."[1]

In the course of operating the center, however, the Dreskins began to notice disturbing changes not only in the children—some previously happy preschoolers beginning to withdraw, lash out or cry incessantly—but also in their interaction with their parents. The parents who were at work all day began to regard the center as having primary responsibility for their children. It dawned on the Dreskins that the changes they were witnessing resulted from center-based care per se, not poor-quality care. "The problem was not with our facility," they wrote. "It was obvious that there was a problem inherent in day care itself, a problem that hung like a dark storm over 'good' and 'bad' day care centers alike." The trouble, they determined, was that day care was disrupting the natural family bonds. "The children were too young to be spending so much time away from their parents. They were like young birds being forced out of the nest and abandoned by their parents before they could fly, their wings undeveloped, unready to carry them out into the world." The Dreskins were "so distressed" by what they observed that they closed down their center.[2]

MOST RESEARCH ON DAY CARE has focused on how it effects the "adjustment" of children to their environment, with very little attention paid to how the center-based environment effects personality and social character. The debate over the effects of extended time in day care on children is strikingly narrow in scope, revolving largely around the questions of whether day care children exhibit symptoms of insecure attachment to their parents, and whether traditional measures of attachment—devised for children raised in a home setting—might be inappropriate indicators for the "different characters" of children who have spent significant time in communal, center-based settings. Almost no one in the field of day care research has asked about the moral or political significance of this new type of social character displayed by the children of day care, and what it might portend for our society.

The disruption of natural family bonds, which the Dreskins witnessed first-hand, profoundly affects children's personalities in ways that may go undetected by studies focusing on achievement and overt behavior. Some researchers and commentators have begun to call attention to the stultifying effects that the overly structured and standardized day care environment has on character. When contrasted with the home, the day care center provides little room for individual expression and development of critical or creative faculties. The child is not given the personal room he or she needs to develop apart from the group, which can result in a conformist mentality and a defective sense of self. Author and social critic Walter Karp wrote that "by virtue of its privacy, the family is the primary shelter of human variety." The family, through the protected environment created in the home, is able to "see to it that the world's standards do not impinge too closely upon the defenseless young and so do not mould them too precisely to the world's imperious demands." According to Karp, the "collective professionalized" environment of day care produces precisely the opposite result: "Instead of protecting the young from the world, such administrative child care would fasten the world's ways on the newborn with a strangler's grip." Not only that, but the security that comes with the unconditional love of the parents in the home environment is replaced, in purchased care, with "the experience of being someone's job."[3]

These changed dynamics of upbringing are likely to result in radically different orientations of character. Ironically, it is the more "protected" environment of the home or a neighborhood setting with parental supervision that allows for greater autonomy and less regimentation in a child's development. This is apparent if we consider that when parents were more profoundly connected to neighborhoods before the dual-income revolution, the neighborhood play of children was much less supervised and adult-organized than it is today when "planned activities" for children are the norm. What is the case at the neighborhood level is also true at the family level. A Smithsonian Institution project in the 1990s set out to discover the sources of human creativity and leadership in early childhood. The study found that the most important influence was a "consistently close parental connection." Adults of strong character also shared such childhood experiences as minimal time spent with peers, and many opportunities to explore the world freely with parental encouragement—neither of these part of the day care world.[4]

In order to maintain control of the children, day care workers repeat the same boring and repetitive activities on a daily basis. By necessity, it is the child who must always conform to the environment, with very little response to individual character, talents or needs. With no time away from the social pressures of the group, children have little opportunity for solitary exploration of their creative potential. The loss of the privacy and spontaneity that are normally afforded in the home environment threatens the development of individual identity.

Differences in the environment of children's upbringing may have more widespread effects than simply altering the character of individual children. Psychologist Brenda Hunter has speculated that the incapacity for commitment characteristic of the culture of divorce may be connected to a decline in normal maternal bonding with children. "We are altering the cultural fabric in this society with the mass exodus of children into day care," she says. "Children who are growing up without a close maternal bond will someday engage in fewer marriages and incur more divorces."[5] Dr. Mohammadreza Hojat, professor of psychiatry at Jefferson Medical College in Philadelphia, warns that day care children "may not develop real concepts of mercifulness and concern for others." As a result of the growing use of group care, "a great many of our children do not gain early, first-hand understanding of concepts such as maternal love, concern, responsiveness, mercifulness, dignity, respect, etc." and therefore fail to internalize these concepts. Dr. Stanley Greenspan offers a similar assessment of how the tenor of society may be altered after much of a generation has spent significant time in day care settings:

> People may gradually become more self-centered and less concerned with others. Thinking may become more polarized, all or nothing, rather than subtle and reflective. Impulsive behavior, helplessness, and depression may increase. The

ability for self-awareness and problem-solving may decrease, as will our capacity to live together and govern ourselves in cohesive communities.[6]

At first glance, Dr. Greenspan's description of fundamental differences in character wrought by experience in collective care may seem at odds with documented increases in "aggressive" and "noncompliant" behavior by day care children. But it is precisely an undeveloped sense of self, and a shortage of the confidence and security usually fostered in the privacy of the family environment, that emerge as lack of self-control, aggressiveness and "selfishness" in social behavior. Jay Belsky has observed that full-time day care "can cause infants to avoid their own parents in a way that may be interpreted as disguised anger, 'a false self.'" It is not unusual, says Belsky, for such children to develop "a manipulative type character."[7]

A collective setting that rewards group-oriented compliance—rather than critical thinking and independent discovery—encourages social skills of manipulation, whether they are devices to seek attention, violent reactions to not getting one's way, or surface conformity and obedience to win approval. It does not encourage the development of a sense of self with internalized rules of conduct that transcend the environment—an inherent sense of right and wrong independent of the child's immediate desires.

Bruno Bettelheim's famous study of the children raised collectively in an Israeli kibbutz bears this out. He observed that children of the kibbutz became oriented toward the group rather than toward individuals. Parents began to exhibit a lack of concern about their own children as the community took over the childrearing responsibilities. Bettelheim also noted that for the children in the kibbutz, conscience did not take the normal form of an internalization of parental authority, but rather an internalization of the community's collective rules. In that context, "morality" became simply a matter of pragmatism. Most of the children were "well adjusted" in the sense that they did not display psychological problems (in part a result of living in a closed community with definite rules), but also absent was any sign that conscience ever came into conflict with what was expedient for getting on in the world. While these children were intensely practical, they showed few eccentric sparks of individuality or originality, rarely stood up against something popular in a group setting, and were singularly uninterested in ideas per se.[8]

Bettelheim concluded that when the parental role becomes weak and institutions and peer groups take over family functions, love becomes separated from discipline and the child's conscience becomes "outer-directed" toward whatever is necessary to fit in with the surrounding environment. Right and wrong are replaced with fashionable and unfashionable. But there was also a darker side: those who found fitting in difficult or impossible had no capacity to find strength and reassurance from an internal code of conduct and thus became alienated. "Adjustment and anomie go together," Bettelheim wrote. "They are the two possibilities for people who lack any inner source of values." The adolescent rage and nihilism that expresses itself in what society regards as the meaningless violence of school shootings may very well have its roots in the undeveloped conscience that results when the normal parent-child relationship is disrupted.

The flip side of the Columbine killers' anomie is the outwardly well-adjusted group of superachieving young "future leaders" at Princeton University profiled by David Brooks in his remarkable article for the *Atlantic Monthly*, "The Organization Kid." These bright, affable undergraduates are on the fast track to success, and they know precisely what they must do to get there. Most have spent their entire lives training to take their place as America's future elite. They are admirably disciplined in pursuing their academic and social goals, and their work ethic is exceptional. Their lives are so closely packed with activities that they have to schedule time just to talk with friends. Yet Brooks finds them strangely lacking in moral character. For all their academic prowess, they are amazingly uninterested in pure ideas, except insofar as mastering them is a practical necessity to achieve the highest possible grade point average. All of their intense activity is oriented toward their own success in life; they have learned what attitudes, studies, acquaintances and accomplishments are needed to make it in American society and they have gone about energetically accumulating them. Even if their aim is to provide the best for their future families and to serve society in some position of influence, they seem to lack any internal code of conduct except that which tells them what it takes to succeed. One doubts whether these people, when faced with dilemmas over doing what success demands versus doing what is right, will have the necessary orientation of conscience to act uprightly.[9]

This trend toward well-adjusted, achievement-oriented young adults who lack any solid inner core of conscience or personal moral criteria was spotted over twenty years ago by David Elkind in his landmark book *The Hurried Child: Growing Up Too Fast Too Soon*. Elkind wrote about an upcoming generation of affluent children that displayed symptoms of having "the feeling of being used, or being exploited by parents, of losing the identity and uniqueness of childhood without just cause." According to Elkind, this syndrome reflected the desire of parents to achieve vicariously through their children, and an increasing tendency to view childhood as a training ground to acquire the necessary skills that advance success in the adult world rather than as a distinct period of growth in maturity, virtue and character that must precede adulthood. This new psychology of the young also reflected the growing trend away from upbringing by parents in the home and toward the more communal settings favored by proponents of "early childhood education."[10]

The emerging pattern that Elkind noticed has now become an ingrained part of popular thinking as a result of the propagandizing efforts of the day care establishment and the pressures on working parents. In a recent book entitled *The Myth of the First Three Years,* John Bruer has pointed out how advocates of early childhood education are using the research on brain development as an excuse for inflicting organized communal activities on young children, with the argument that they enhance skills (and future test scores).[11] Just beneath the surface of the trendy claim that neuroscience proves the necessity of stimulating a child's brain properly during the first three years—lest he or she be permanently stunted intellectually—is the idea that childrearing consists of getting young children on track early for their future roles as academic stars and chief executive officers in a knowledge-based economy. Whether they will be good spouses, parents or citizens is another question.

No wonder proponents of greater public investment in day care are beginning to argue that center-based care should be viewed essentially as preschool or "early childhood education." Danielle Ewen of the Children's Defense Fund was explicit about the analogy in a *Newsweek* story: "Preschool is child care. Child care is preschool."[12] As Kay Hymowitz has noted, however, this equation doesn't mean that day care is "education in the humanistic or civic sense; it is all business; it is school in the vocational sense. The point is to train babies, yes—for the workplace." It is a very narrow conception of education that does not acknowledge its moral importance in molding character, and the logical conclusion of such small-mindedness is, in Hymowitz's vivid words, "the absurdity of seeing a toothless infant batting at his crib gym as an executive-in-training."[13] A mindset that regards human-worth as limited to income-earning potential is not likely to have much appreciation for the family as the school of character.

IDENTIFYING THE GOOD OF THE ECONOMY with the good of the family is inherently problematic as concerns the interests of parents, and it is a relatively novel view. In terms of family welfare, economic growth is a double-edged sword. It is undoubtedly true that economic downturns have negative effects on the family—for obvious reasons. Typical effects of a recession—unemployment, loss of financial security, falling standards of living and the like—put strains on marriages and families that aren't felt when times are good. Less obvious may be the fact that growth in the Gross Domestic Product is not, in itself, something that automatically redounds to the family's benefit. Indeed, it can even be a gauge of familial and societal breakdown. The growth in divorce, the use of commercial day care, recourse to fast food instead of eating at home, more money spent on deterring crime and repairing the damage it causes, and the various and sundry ways in which traditional family functions are farmed out to the market economy (not to mention the booming pornography and gambling industries)—all these phenomena show up on the national books as "growth." So do depletion of natural resources and expenditures on cleaning up the environment. The GDP is simply a measure of transactions, of money changing hands. When pursued as a good in itself, without relation to the nature of the transactions taking place, GDP growth is bound to lead to a disordered economic policy—and a disordered society.

Illustrating that the family isn't always the beneficiary of economic growth, an *Atlantic Monthly* article points to "The Index of Leading Cultural Indicators," a much-cited catalogue of social and family decline produced by William J. Bennett in 1993. "The strange fact that jumps out from Bennett's grim inventory of crime, divorce, mass-media addiction, and the rest," the authors write, "is that much of it actually adds to the GDP." Indeed, high divorce rates translate into lots of market activity such as lawyers' bills, second households and so on; high crime rates mean a booming security industry; children watching inordinate amounts of television instead of interacting with parents means a booming "kiddie market" and "teen market" of consumer products (adding more than $200 billion to the GDP).[14] The lesson for families is clear: the conventional measurements of growth usually held up as a gauge of economic vibrancy can mask all sorts of social and family pathologies. We always need to keep sight of the principle that the economy exists to serve people (nurtured and sustained in families), not vice versa. To a large extent, America has lost its moorings in this respect, as the late cultural critic Christopher Lasch pointed out: "Instead of building our economy around the needs of families, we have allowed economic imperatives to govern the structure of the family, the school, and every other agency of cultural transmission."[15] One result of this reordering has been that, in this era of the "highest standard of living in the world's history," many parents today don't feel able to spare time to care for their own children, as even impoverished parents did until relatively recently.

When the energies and attention of the culture are focused on the marketplace, the social and economic contributions of the home—particularly the parents' role in bringing up their children—tend to be regarded as irrelevant. The devaluing of motherhood has affected not only married mothers' estimation of the value to the family of rearing children at home, but that of married fathers as well. It has now become culturally acceptable for husbands to pressure their wives to leave the children in day care and get a job for the sake of the family finances.

The debate over day care will not address the fundamental needs of families as long as it revolves around the so-

called "needs of the economy." Here, the converging interests of feminist supporters of a day care regime, business
leaders and proponents of an expanded federal government
become apparent. Feminists and other day care advocates
commonly maintain that the "needs of the economy" or the
"needs of the labor force" demand the workforce participation of married mothers. In the same way, the "needs of government spending" can only be sustained by the larger tax
base that comes with married mothers in the workplace.

This has been explicitly acknowledged by the Swedes, cited
as the "model" welfare society by so many who promote
government subsidies for day care. The Swedish government
concluded that "the gain which the State makes from the
taxes paid by the working women would be greater than the
cost of [funding] the day care system," and that the welfare
society of Sweden "can be financed only by taxes from a
labor market in which almost everyone is working and paying taxes."[16] That is fine with the former chairman of the
socialist Swedish People's Party, who was stunningly direct
in spelling out the party's agenda of shifting individual alle-
giances from the family to the state:

> The parental monopoly cannot be broken solely by indirect
> measures—the State must intervene directly, by, for exam-
> ple, taking the children from the parents during part of their
> growing up years.... It is best for the children and society
> that a universal and compulsory preschool program become
> clearly indoctrinating, thus enabling society to intervene
> more directly when it comes to the children's values and
> attitudes.[17]

While most American feminist advocates of day care do
not call for the alienation of children from their parents so
as to reorient "children's values and attitudes," the push for
a system of publicly supported day care certainly reflects an
underlying hostility to the notion of parents being primarily

responsible for their children's spiritual, intellectual and emotional formation. Their public arguments for center-based,
commercial care rely more on the convenience to families
of "professionalizing" the care of preschoolers. (Because
"child care professionals" are in charge, parents with access
to high-quality care can rest easy about safety, hygiene,
health, nutrition, education and play.) As at-home parenting becomes increasingly uneconomical, it is portrayed as
less desirable than the alternative—even though it is what
most parents want. Since center-based care is a commercial
endeavor, it is depicted as more reliably consistent than both
parents and relatives, who might be sick or otherwise unavailable in a pinch. It is a "service" that working parents require
due to the hectic demands of modern life.

Christopher Lasch cut to the heart of this conceit when he
pointed out that although "the expansion of professional
authority at the expense of the family has been justified on
the grounds that the best way to 'help' the family is to relieve
it of its responsibilities," the true result "has been to weaken
the ties between the generations, to reduce the emotional inten-
sity of the parent-child connection, to deprive children of direct
access to adult experience, and to produce a generation of
young people who are morally and emotionally at sea, lacking any sense of participation in their culture's tradition or in
its ongoing development." With his usual perceptiveness, Lasch
concluded that even though it pretends to speak for the interests and serve the needs of the family, the day care industry
"actually weakens its authority at every point."[18]

At one time, liberals would have been the first to recognize that the good of the economy is distinct from the well-
being of families, and to fight against the intrusion of the
market into the sacrosanct domestic sphere. In fact, an earlier women's movement did just that. Before Betty Friedan
and the new feminism equated careerism with progress for
women, protecting mothers in the home from having to

work out of economic necessity was central to both the thinking and the political agenda of the early-twentieth-century women's movement.[19]

The triumph of contemporary feminism affected liberalism in profound ways, not least of which was a new identification of women's interests with independence from husbands and family, and a correspondingly greater dependence on corporations and government. Traditionally, American women had accepted placement of children in day care only in emergency circumstances, and only "until the mother could be restored to her rightful place in the home," in the words of social historian Margaret Steinfels. "Day care was not a service for the normal."[20] But the older notion that mothers' interests required some protection of the family from the intrusions of the market economy began to break down with the new feminism's attack on that domestic realm as precisely what women needed to be liberated from.

Leaving aside the question of whether women themselves benefit in being liberated from the domestic economy and becoming more reliant on corporations and government, this transfer of loyalties demanded by the new feminism has had definite effects on cultural values. The interdependence and self-sacrifice associated with family life at home are less esteemed than ever, while the individual achievement and temporary, self-interested relationships of the marketplace have been elevated to the level of preeminent values in the popular culture. As the marketplace relationships of the day care center and the elder care facility gain ground over the mutual interdependence of generations in the domestic sphere, the bonds between family members become less meaningful and family life itself becomes more strained. The breakdown of the family in the United States is not only the result of changed social mores, but is also closely related to the notion that the love of family members can be replaced by purchased care in the marketplace.

Pushing for more provision of on-site day care by corporations, Senator Barbara Mikulski reflected this mentality when she argued that "if the private sector is enlightened enough to provide slots for employees to park their cars, it can provide slots for employees' children."[21] But the idea that "slots for children" at the workplace can substitute for a parent's care is ultimately absurd, even in economic terms. As G. K. Chesterton remarked over eighty years ago, "If people cannot mind their own business, it cannot possibly be more economical to pay them to mind each other's business, and still less to mind each other's babies." In the name of efficiency, Chesterton noted, day care advocates were ignoring the plain fact that the natural family system is "economical" precisely because it is outside of the economy: "Ultimately, [they] are arguing that a woman should not be a mother to her own baby, but a nursemaid to somebody else's baby. But it will not work, even on paper. We cannot all live by taking in each other's washing, especially in the form of pinafores."[22] But at a 1997 White House Conference on Child Care, California child care consultant Patty Siegel complained that "the child care crisis is so acute that child care workers in many areas of the country are unable to find adequate day care for their own children."[23] Thus has Chesterton's *reductio ad absurdum* become a reasonable argument.

Neither can a system of purchased care for children adequately replace the parents' role as legal guardians. Zealous day care proponent Sandra Scarr discovered, to her dismay, that when parents entrust their own flesh and blood to the vicissitudes of purchased care, "society" cannot be relied upon to protect a child. When her own eighteen-month-old daughter was beaten by a babysitter, Scarr was told by police that no one could be prosecuted without witnesses. When Scarr wrote that "no one was there to prevent the abuse or to testify about it," she seemed oblivious to the irony that she was, in essence, complaining about her own absence.[24]

The radical feminists have always been aware, however, that their social experiment of mandating equality of outcome in the job market would ultimately run up against the reality of mothers' actual choices for home and family. Full statistical equality in economic and political life for women can be achieved only with the abandonment of motherhood as traditionally understood. The problem, from the feminist perspective, is that women will not abandon that traditional role if left to their own devices. The late Simone de Beauvoir, one of the most significant intellectual influences on modern feminism, bluntly argued that "women should not have the choice [to stay home], precisely because if there is such a choice, too many women will make that one."[25] Rather than reflecting popular demand, the early support of radical feminists for government funding of day care was based on this very acknowledgement that workforce parity could not be achieved without the implementation of strong cultural and economic incentives.

It would also be necessary, according to the new feminism, to overcome the traditional division of labor between spouses. As long as mothers were the primary providers of child care, statistical equity in the world of politics and business would remain elusive. Feminist writer Nancy Chodorow insisted that shared childrearing responsibilities between the spouses is an absolute necessity if society is to overcome "the sexual division of labor in which women mother."[26] The 1996 Beijing Conference on Women echoed this theme, calling on governments to "change attitudes that reinforce the division of labor based on gender in order to promote the concept of shared family responsibility for work in the home, particularly in relation to children and elder care."[27] Another zealous advocate of radical feminism, the former president of Iceland, made it clear that the political agenda of day care proponents is not so much a means of providing parents with the options they demand as it is a strategy for achieving equal power between the sexes in public life:

As long as the private sphere remains largely women's concern, they will be much less available than men for positions
of responsibility in economic and political life.

Among the strategies, mention might be made of the gen-
eralization of parental leave, shared between mothers and
fathers, greater availability of childcare facilities, care for the
old and encouragement for men to participate in housework.[28]

Since the new feminist version of women's empowerment
requires all women to pursue careers and be economically
independent of their husbands, it cannot abide the realities
of motherhood. Pregnancy and the responsibilities of motherhood by necessity affect the workforce participation of
women, and not just because they are unfortunate incon-
veniences imposed on females by an oppressive nature and
an oppressive society. Most women freely choose to scale
back their workforce participation because they want to invest
themselves in raising their children. In most cases, however,
it is their "economic dependence" on their husbands that
allows them to make the choice of motherhood. That dependence is exactly what feminist ideology seeks to make imprac-
tical, if not to abolish outright.

THEIR VIEW OF WOMEN'S EMANCIPATION puts feminist supporters of day care in the strange position of pushing to increase
the number of children who must lead regimented lives.
They lobby for public schools and businesses to include day
care programs for preschoolers, push for longer school years
and mandatory summer school, and want to lower the age
of kindergarten. Not only that, they seek greater government
intervention into family life to insure that parents are raising their children correctly in the home. "Every home and
family should be taught, through parenting education and
family visitation by social service intermediaries, how to raise

children," insists Senator Hillary Clinton. "This would begin in the prenatal stages and continue through childhood."[29]

The philosophy that seeks government supervision of child-rearing is not just a feminist fantasy; it is also practically orthodox thinking in the social service establishment. Wisconsin's superintendent of public instruction argued in 1993 that the "definition of education" must "include a child's continuing intellectual, physical, emotional and social development and well-being." He further insisted that Wisconsin's schools must provide "full-time preschool child care, before- and after-school child care, parent training . . . early childhood education programs and health, mental health and social services" as well as "home visits to parents." Illinois pro-family groups narrowly defeated a bill that would have allowed the state board of education to send state employees into homes of "parents of children in the period of life from birth to kindergarten" to supervise and train those parents without their consent. In Missouri, the Parents As Teachers program already sends social service workers into more than 150,000 homes to instruct mothers and fathers in government-approved methods of parenting.[30]

Despite the dearth of evidence that such intervention has any positive effects on the school performance or social development of children, it remains a priority for the education establishment. One of the fullest expressions of the interventionist mindset was given by Anne Mitchell of Bank Street College when she envisioned a "complete intervention . . . for at-risk young children and their families" which "would be a comprehensive package that combines full-day, year-round early childhood programs that are in the best senses both custodial and educational, with parent education/ family support programs that have a strong employment training component."[31] Remarkably, those who support government intrusion into parenting decisions and child care arrangements commonly depict opponents of such schemes as "anti-child" or "anti-women." Opposition to subsidies for day care is portrayed as an interference in the free choices of mothers—to work. "Keeping government out of child care support and regulation," argues Sandra Scarr, "is a subterfuge for opposition to women in the labor force and child care provisions that might allow more mothers to work more comfortably."

It is in this context that one should view comments like those of Senator Christopher Dodd that the "early childhood education" of center-based day care is desirable from "the point that the child leaves the womb."[32] The importance of such "education" is not that it helps at-risk children, in other words, but that it undermines traditional motherhood, family life and the influence of parents on their children. Infant day care proponents E. Belle Evans and George E. Saia admit as much when they bemoan the fact that when mothers raise their children at home, "the mother's values, wishes, needs, desires, and expectations are readily imposed on the developing child, who often becomes a symbiotic extension of the mother through whom she attempts to fulfill her own unrealized ambitions." The authors argue that this is "especially destructive to the child who often must live out his mother's unfulfilled dreams rather than realize his own identity." On the other hand, children who are put in day care as infants "may enjoy a better chance of developing their own individuality in a child-care center where the personal emotional investment of many adults is dissipated rather than in a highly intense one-to-one mother-child relationship in the home."[33] This, be it noted, runs exactly counter to what other researchers have concluded about the value of one-to-one care in the privacy of the home for the formation of an independent personality.

Another basic element in the attack on motherhood is the school of academic feminists who advocate "androgynous" parenting. Going beyond the well-worn notion that all differences in behavior between the sexes are "socially con-structed," with no biological basis, these androgyny advo-cates have another, more important, goal: the establishment as a social norm of the dual-career family that utilizes day care and shares the remaining parental duties interchange-ably. The idea of 50/50 parenting is that moms and dads should each do 50 percent of the income earning in the paid workforce and 50 percent of whatever child care is necessary in the home (excepting, perhaps, shared breastfeeding respon-sibilities). Both parents should take equal amounts of time off from work for "parental" leave to take care of childrear-ing tasks. The fact that the vast majority of parents prefer to arrange things so that one parent earns the family income while the other stays home to care for the children is seen as an unfortunate result of social conditioning and the lack of adequate, affordable day care. The idea that mothers play a uniquely nurturing role in the care of young children is completely denied.

In fact, some "progressive" academics now claim that there is no such thing as maternal instinct. Before the modern age, according to Edward Shorter, a historian in the Faculty of Medicine at the University of Toronto, maternal affection simply did not exist. Shorter penned the highly influential *The Making of the Modern Family* (1975), in which he argued that the close-knit family of 1950s American television pro-grams was a historical novelty. In previous ages, "mothers viewed the development and happiness of infants younger than two with indifference," he wrote.[34] Even though such theories have been thoroughly debunked by real historians, they continue to hold sway.

In fact, twenty-five years after first being asserted, Shorter's contentions now seem relatively mild. In her book *Mother Nature: A History of Mothers, Infants, and Natural Selection,* feminist writer Sara Blaffer Hrdy makes the bold claim that mothers have historically been just as likely to murder their infant children as to nurture them. A professor emeritus of anthropology at the University of California at Davis, Hrdy claims that older popular notions of "mother-love" are male social constructs meant to maintain political power, in which the "high-status male primate [is] intent on controlling where, when, and how females belonging to his group reproduce." Now that we no longer take for granted "the centuries-old view of self-sacrificing motherhood," writes Hrdy, we are able to see that "wherever women have both control over their reproductive opportunities and a chance to better themselves, women opt for well-being and economic security over having more children."[35]

The feminist claim that motherhood is just an oppressive social construct is more influential among opinion makers in the media and academia than most parents realize, and it has significantly affected family policy and corporate practice. It has also had a major impact on the sociological researchers who study the effects of day care on children, many of whom now posit that exclusive mother-care is a twentieth-century creation and that the historical norm has been multiple caregivers. The truth, however, is that even in aboriginal societies in which mothers do share caregiving, they share it with relatives who have known the children throughout their lives. This is simply not comparable to the current commercial day care regime, where children are in the care of strangers who have no blood ties or long-term commitment to them. As Dr. Stanley Greenspan has written, "the current social experiment, where middle- and upper-middle-income families who can afford it use institutions outside the home to care for their infants and toddlers is a significant departure from very recent history." It was often "the nannies or nursemaids of the past, who were stable figures for many years in the families who could afford them," who "did the consistent, one-on-one nurturing" that the revisionists deny was taking place.[36]

THE SYMPATHY OF RADICAL FEMINISM with the tendency of encroaching capitalism to replace family bonds with the market loyalties of workplace and paycheck has not often been recognized. But it has always been an integral aspect of the strain of feminism that regards the abolition of traditional motherhood and family relationships as the key to progress for women. A century ago, the prophetic Charlotte Perkins Gilman—almost unique in an era when the women's movement was identified with maternalism and opposition to mothers' labor force participation—asserted that industrial society "was freeing the individual, old and young, from enforced association on family lines," which would allow for "free association on social lines" and "wide individual intercourse" without the burden of family ties. Gilman argued that the family as an institution was in its death throes, and that "the lines of social relation today are mainly industrial." A new order of loyalties had to be forged: "As our industrial organization has grown to the world-encircling intricacies of today ... the unerring response of the soul to social needs has given us a new kind of loyalty—*loyalty to our work.*"[37]

Modern feminist advocates of "big business socialism" echo Gilman's views quite closely. Judy Heymann points out, in *The Widening Gap: Why America's Working Families Are in Jeopardy and What Can Be Done About It,* that "the revolutionary movement of men and women into the industrial and post-industrial labor force has transformed the United States." Since, in her view, the exodus of mothers into the workforce cannot be reversed, Heymann suggests that all preschoolers be educated and cared for by the government on a scale equal to the public education provided for five- to eighteen-year-olds. She also urges a lengthening of the school day and school year for older children, paid parental leave insurance for all working adults, government subsidies

for care of the elderly, and greater public funding of trans-
portation so that family members can more easily travel
between various care centers.

In *Care and Equality: Inventing a New Family Politics,* Mona
Harrington calls for society to "explicitly link economics and
the function of caregiving" in centers outside the home
through the establishment of a new system funded with public monies. All this is necessary because of "the *unfair* allocation to women of the major costs of caregiving." Praising
former president Clinton's use of the term "corporate citi-
zen" and his recognition of the responsibilities of the business world in creating a new family order, Harrington urges
liberals to establish "a society-wide system of good family
care on terms of equality for women." Those family functions that remain, in her view, must be socialized. Her agenda
includes: extending the Family and Medical Leave Act to
cover all employees and to mandate paid leave; "joint cor-
porate-government contributions" to create a "guaranteed
annual income" for every household; high-quality day care
and bigger tax credits for parents who use it; support for early
childhood care and education as well as the expansion of
after-school programs; subsidies to insure better training and
higher salaries for day care workers; and higher levels of funding for elder care centers. All this, argues Harrington, is necessary to institute a "new politics of social responsibility."[38]

Feminist Theda Skocpol acknowledges that it is in the
enlightened self-interest of corporations to contribute to the
weakening of family bonds, since marriage and parenting
get in the way of the most efficient allocation of labor. But
corporate capitalism, she insists, is perfectly compatible with
the dual-income family—as long as government provides
adequate social supports for the worker bees. "It is a myth
that vibrant market capitalism and adequate social supports
for working families cannot go hand in hand," she writes.
To sustain the new family order, government and business

alike must "increase the stake of people of all ages—and generations—in national social programs." Skocpol's social support system would include universal health insurance, paid family leave, "repeated increases in the minimum wage" and "a national system of subsidized care with state support going to both institutions and families." Because today "participation in the wage-employment system is universally understood as desirable for all adults, men and women, mothers and fathers alike," Skocpol concludes that "it will be necessary to revalue national government as an instrument for addressing broadly shared needs in the name of democratically shared values." Only when families give up the small bits of autonomy they still possess to the corporate state will "work and family . . . mesh more smoothly."[39]

But support for this new, big business–friendly nanny state to replace the traditional family at home is by no means restricted to the academic left. It also happens to be the cutting edge of management theory in "conservative" business schools. Stewart Friedman and Jeffrey Greenhaus, professors of business management at, respectively, the Wharton School of the University of Pennsylvania and Drexel University, argue persuasively that corporate capitalism as we know it today is neither socially conservative nor a bulwark against family breakdown. Quite the contrary: since corporations thrive in social turmoil—claiming the loyalties of workers without family and neighborhood roots to get in the way— the business professors urge America to "keep the *revolution* going," because "the struggle for the creation of new and more varied lifestyle options is far from over." To further this revolution, the old notion of "hierarchies" within families must finally be put to rest, and Americans "must be prepared to make the most of the *brave new world*" of corporate-based (rather than family-based) loyalties. This *"workplace revolution"* is a necessary result of capitalism's genius for "creative destruction." Since "women seem to be more skilled" than men in the qualities so desired in the new economy, such as handling ambiguity, multitasking and building personal networks, they must participate more fully in the *"brave new world* of twenty-first century careers." (Emphases added.) The authors even argue for "innovative summer camps" for children in order to "open [their] minds to challenging the traditional gender roles," a necessary preparation for the postfamily reordering of loyalties. Professors Friedman and Greenhaus single out Hillary Rodham Clinton's book *It Takes a Village* for special praise on account of its "powerful message" that "each of us—society as a whole—bears responsibility for all children, even other people's children." The policy measures that the professors call for in order to bring forth their "brave new world" are almost identical to those of the gender feminists: government subsidies to "significantly increase the quality and affordability of child care for working parents," strengthened family leave laws, and more recruiting, training and pay for a professional class of child care workers, all accomplished with state funds.[40]

The idea that parental responsibilities and child care in the home are obstacles to business efficiency has also made considerable inroads into the corporate boardrooms of major American companies. At a conference on Family and Work in 1996, Randall Tobias, former CEO of Eli Lilly, sneered at the "outdated" view that male heads of families should be able to earn enough to enable a mother to raise preschool children in the home. This antiquated notion, he argued, is the reason that some companies still maintain personnel policies "based on Ozzie and Harriet." Because such traditional family structures apply to only about 18 percent of employees, according to Tobias, companies need to take on an increasingly paternal role. Eli Lilly, in addition to on-site day care, has a cafeteria that prepares take-home dinners four nights a week, a dry cleaning facility and a twenty-four-hour counseling service for its employees. Tobias emphasized the

bottom-line benefits that the company reaps from such progressive policies, asserting that "the child care facility will
benefit not only the families that use it, but all our employees, stockholders, customers—all who benefit from the undi-
vided attention of our employees." Because of increased
conflict at home and family-related stress, many other companies, such as Marriott in Atlanta, have begun to offer professional counseling from a staff of full-time social workers.
Human resources director Donna Klein explained that Marriott had decided to retain social workers on staff because
some managers were spending an inordinate amount of their
time counseling employees with family problems.[41]

Meanwhile, policies that offer parents more flexibility in
scheduling and allow them to spend more time at home are
little used in most companies. The feminist lobby resists any
discussion of proposals such as flex time and telecommuting, in the belief that because more mothers would take
advantage of them than fathers, they would slow the movement toward gender equality in career achievement. Suggestions that employers should recognize the existence of two
types of female employees in their work policies, those for
whom career comes first and those for whom family obligations come first, are mocked as singling out women for a
"mommy track" that hampers their careers. Any values that
are seen to be in conflict with the professional advancement
of women in the money economy are rejected, no matter
how popular among the rank and file of working women.[42]

Large, publicly held firms have another reason to advance
the feminist agenda in the economic sphere—precisely
because it weakens and dissolves families and the domestic
life. In one particularly illustrative example from a few years
ago, the McDonald's Corporation made a grant to the
National Organization for Women, reasoning no doubt that
the furtherance of NOW's agenda would mean more business from parents and children at fast-food restaurants.

The new paternalist attitude on the part of corporations was justified by Robert Allen, former CEO of AT&T, in the promotional literature of the 1996 Family and Work Conference.

> We have not traditionally linked the well-being of children to the success of business or the governance of nations. Yet increasingly we're acknowledging that upheavals in the American family aren't self-contained—they intersect with business and economic circles and loop into the social fabric of this nation. As a society, we assume a large affiliation—one that implies, not just family ties, but added obligations.[43]

What is so striking about Mr. Allen's formulation is that the well-being of children is accorded importance insofar as it affects "the success of business or the governance of nations." This reflects a reversal of the concern with an expanding commercialism that the old family-wage regime was erected to guard against: the intrusion into the domestic sphere of industrial or business pressures, to the detriment of family welfare. It tells us that we have experienced a true cultural revolution in the relationship of work and family. The only question today is whether "upheavals in the American family" impinge on the success of business, or whether business imperatives intrude on the sanctity of the family.

In fact, many businesses are knowingly using "family-friendly" policies as a way of dissolving family loyalties. In a remarkable document entitled "The Five Stages of Family-Friendly Companies," Ellen Galinsky's Families and Work Institute outlined the ways in which corporations can slowly take over family functions:

STAGE I: "Overcoming an initial resistance to address these issues," companies can "offer a child care resource and referral service to help employees find child care, or provide assistance in paying for child care."

STAGE II: Companies "broaden their scope" in addressing work-family issues in a "coordinated, comprehensive effort" to "expand the definition of 'family.'" Strategies include adding "elder care resource and referral services" and "parental leave for mothers AND fathers."

STAGE III: Companies shift the focus "from work-family to work-life" by beginning to address the needs of workers more directly. A priority is placed on "removing mixed messages within the organization" and "making the organizational culture more family-friendly."

STAGE IV: In the interests of "business productivity," companies are made to "recognize that they can profit by looking at the whole person." Companies show their employees that work and family obligations do not conflict with one another by moving away "from the notion of work-life conflict toward work-life synergy."

STAGE V: Finally, employers achieve full family-friendliness by "linking community with company" and building "a sense of community in the workplace." Companies also "promote and provide training for skills (such as conflict resolution) needed at work, at home, and in community participation."

From the perspective of most parents struggling to find more time for their children, such a "family-friendly" future is likely to seem pretty ghastly. But this "brave new world" seems equally desired by radical feminists and the Fortune 500. The striking similarity between the two in thinking about the family raises some interesting questions about what it is, exactly, that the modern feminist movement has achieved. In contrast to the maternalist women's movement of the first part of the twentieth century, modern "careerist" feminism fits comfortably into the corporate-state economy. As a result of the new feminism's success in achieving its goal of empowered professional women, the entire adult population—rather than just half of it—is now expected to participate in the labor force. As author Charles Siegel puts it, "because of the modern women's movement, we have moved from the 1950s organization man to today's organization person."[44] The feminist left's continuing attack on repressive "patriarchal structures" seems hopelessly irrelevant today, when it is corporations, not husbands, who hold real power in society. The feminist agenda—especially the establishment of day care as a social norm—simply puts more power in the same hands. That's precisely why so many CEOs and professors of business support day care. But to a generation that has grown up with working parents, an impoverished home life, and the empty vulgarity of consumerist culture, the feminist fight against the "patriarchal" family looks to be not only anachronistic, but a large contributor to the problem.

IN THE FACE OF THE STRANGE but powerful alliance of feminists and the Business Roundtable, who can be relied upon to defend the interests of children and families? Even though the vast majority of parents are opposed to day care for young children as the norm, it must be acknowledged that under the influence of such powerful financial and social incentives, it will be difficult to reverse the trends in the direction of center-based care for preschool children. Parents have relatively little influence on family policymakers compared with the other players featured in this book.

But there are also indications of a parental revolt brewing against the day care establishment. In the last decade there has been a remarkable sea-change in sentiment among parents, a growing reaction against both the commercialization of traditional family functions and the careerist mentality that seeks personal fulfillment through professional achievement at the expense of the family. It is just possible that the prospect of a society composed of the children of constantly working parents raised by a professional class of day care workers in technocratic, amoral institutions for the benefit of the corporate-socialist state will be the last straw that causes parents to reclaim their prerogatives and recognize that strengthening the vitality of family life in the home is the key to their survival in every sense of the word.

SEVEN

How Parents Can Take Back Parenting

For each of the major political parties, there are different reasons to disregard the sentiments of parents when it comes to child care policy. For most Democrats, it is not simply a matter of close ties with the day care establishment, but also a worldview that regards child-rearing as something best carried out by professionals. That mindset was well expressed by longtime day care proponent Senator Edward Kennedy over twenty years ago when he declared that "child care in modern American life is not just a bonus for the poor, but a necessity for families of all types and conditions—intact families, single parent families, families at every step of the income ladder."[1] It was also reflected in the phrase made famous by Hillary Rodham Clinton when she was First Lady: "It takes a village to raise a child." A more candid rendering of her philosophy might have been "it takes a government-subsidized day care worker to raise a child."

Among leading conservative economists (and some liberals as well), the day care regime serves the notion that the economy demands a fully employed, highly flexible and increasingly productive workforce, which in turn necessitates the participation of mothers with young children—even at the cost of having to make provisions for the nonparental care of those children. Bush administration economic advisor Martin Feldstein, arguing for the president's tax reform proposals, wrote in the *Wall Street Journal,*

By lowering marginal tax rates, Mr. Bush's plan will change taxpayers' behavior in ways that make up for much of the revenue loss. . . . [It will] induce people to work and earn more. Married women are particularly sensitive to lower rates, responding with higher labor-force participation rates and greater average hours of work per week.[2]

The constituency of married mothers with young children can wield more influence inside the GOP than it does within the Democratic Party, but by and large, Republicans have shown little understanding of the economic dynamics involved in the increasing pressure on families who want to raise their own children at home. A perfect illustration of the GOP's tin ear on the issue of work and family is the case of Jane Swift, who, as Republican lieutenant governor of Massachusetts, got into considerable political difficulty for using statehouse aides as babysitters for her infant daughter. Swift seemed oblivious to the fact that the vast majority of working parents can't rely on employees to run errands and help with child care so that they can spend "quality time" with their children without risking their jobs. Completely unrepentant, she huffed, "If I have to work twelve- or fifteen-hour days, I am not going to allow the media or anyone else . . . to prevent me from spending time with my daughter."[3] Apparently it never occurred to Ms. Swift that tax policies supported by her own administration worked to the disadvantage of a majority of her own constituents who struggled to spend more time with their own children and raise them at home.

Even many self-professed "family values" conservatives seem unconcerned about the fact that—contrary to the trend in other industrialized countries—American families are devoting more and more time to marketplace labor. According to the International Labor Organization, the average American is now putting in another whole week of work per year compared with just ten years ago, and one hundred hours a year more than even the average Japanese worker. Americans "want to progress, to move on to the next level," explained Lawrence Johnson, the economist in charge of the study. "To do that they're putting in more hours."[4] Despite appearances of greater prosperity, families have had to devote a substantially higher number of hours to the labor market in the last thirty years just to stay even. According to one study, wives worked almost twice as many hours in 1991 as they did twenty years earlier, and the combined number of hours both spouses devoted to household work (including child care) sank by one-third. The same study showed that after 1985 the "ability of a single wage laborer to provide sufficient economic support for the family" had eroded considerably, and the authors forecast that the wage gap between males in dual-earner and single-earner families would continue to grow in the foreseeable future, making the traditional arrangement of one parent taking care of the children at home "an increasingly untenable option for most families."[5]

Indeed, the standard libertarian-conservative approach to free market economics scarcely acknowledges the vital contributions that families make to the economy by investing time and effort in raising their children. The theoretical roots of this omission have been summed up by economist John Mueller's idea: they tend to subscribe to the "stork theory of economics." The lack of support for parents at home and the favorable view of the movement of mothers into the workplace, says Mueller, are based on the notion that the fundamental social and economic unit of society is "a curious creature called the individual," who is delivered "by a large economic stork" as a full-grown adult. Mueller's metaphor shows how irrational are libertarian assumptions that individual adult workers do not cost anything to produce, and that "affecting the number of individuals in the population is not possible." In reality, Mueller points out, not only do government-imposed tax burdens on married couples with children affect family size, but to bring a baby to adulthood "requires a huge investment of resources, mostly by the household." The way the tax system treats that investment is crucial; yet under the reigning "stork theory," only investment in nonhuman capital (buildings, machines and such) is seen as productive. Parents at home are regarded as "totally useless" because the existing ways of categorizing the economic activity of adults—"work" and "leisure"—are inadequate to account for the even more crucial economic activity of childrearing. Therefore parents at home are "totally useless individuals" who "devote all their time to leisure: for example, tending household pets called children."

This view is strikingly similar to the radical feminist idea of full-time parents as worthless, and it makes proposals to expand the current subsidies for day care seem a rational way of taking those worthless individuals out of the home and turning them into productive workers. On any other analysis, the favorable treatment accorded to parents who choose to put their children in commercial day care is plainly inequitable, especially considering the unpopularity of such special treatment with the vast majority of parents.

The fact that many "pro-family" conservatives do not recognize the anti-family implications of some of their economic policies was perhaps best encapsulated by none other than Ronald Reagan. In a speech given during his presidency, Reagan praised stay-at-home moms by saying that "unlike Sweden ... the mothers of America have managed to avoid becoming just so many more cogs in the wheels of commerce."[6] At the same time, however, he pointed proudly to the fact that his economic policies had created so many jobs as to give the United States the highest "employment ratio" in the world—without recognizing that a higher employment ratio means that more mothers are working.[7]

IN SPITE OF ALL THE INCENTIVES and perks granted by government and the private sector, families continue to resist putting their children in institutional day care, and show inventiveness in finding ways to avoid it. After a seemingly inexorable increase over the past three decades in the percentage of married mothers with preschool children who work full-time, this trend seems to have leveled off, according to the latest statistics. And a 2002 Census Bureau report indicates that 53 percent of children younger than five are still cared for primarily by their parents, while the percentage of those cared for by relatives still exceeds those cared for in organized facilities.[8]

A rational approach to reform in this area must acknowledge the incentives that have skewed the child care market in the direction of nonparental care. The soaring tax burden on families with children has obviously also played an enormous part in distorting the rational child care choices of parents. To get an idea of just how hard parents have been hit by increasing taxes, consider that in 1948 the average family with children paid only 3 percent of its income in federal taxes; today, the average family pays almost 25 percent of its income in federal taxes alone.[9] One recent study calculated that the average married couple pays *46 percent* of its income to the government in the form of federal, state and local taxes, both direct and indirect.[10] Marriage and children once served as the most important tax shelters, but this is no longer the case since Congress and inflation have dismantled the family-friendly tax code of the baby boom period of 1946 to 1963. Policymakers could go a long way toward reassembling that pro-family system if they were convinced of the political and economic benefits that could be reaped.

But first we must be clear-sighted enough to dismiss some of the sillier notions that have governed public policy thinking on the issue of child care—clichés that have become fixtures of the debate, to the detriment of reasonable solutions. Prominent among them is the idea that the rise in the workforce commitment of mothers with children of preschool age—and the corresponding rise in the use of commercial, center-based care for those children—is an "inexorable" trend, which we are powerless to affect. Day care advocates have long used the claim of inevitability when pressing for greater subsidies and investment of public funds. But the argument is, simply put, nonsense. Social and political trends are always subject to human intervention, and when the vast majority of people find those trends repugnant, they can be reversed. That cultural forces and financial pressures are moving us in the direction of the nonparental care of children says nothing about whether government should act to alleviate or assist those trends.

Another notion that must be dispelled is that if government did *not* generously subsidize the day care system, it would take away the freedom of mothers with young children to work. This commonly heard argument inverts the meaning of words in a truly Orwellian fashion. Publicly funding and subsidizing day care, far from achieving a net gain in free choice, forces families that are already making financial sacrifices so that one parent can be home with the children to pay for benefits for other families, often wealthier, who have chosen to put their children in purchased care— the least popular option for most parents. Such a policy diminishes rather than expands parental choice and child care options.

It is true, however, that a fundamental decision must be made about the direction of child care policy, because a system of widespread nonparental day care cannot be sustained without massive government subsidy, which necessarily works to the great disadvantage of parents making sacrifices to invest time in their children's upbringing. We must determine how we want our children to be raised. We can either fund day care centers and subsidize purchased care or we can make it easier for parents to be parents and care for their own children. In making this fundamental political choice, we should keep in mind that the most interested party, namely the children themselves, are unable to lobby for their own best interests—the fundamental right to be cared for, if possible, by their parents in the home environment.

If we acknowledge that parental care of children in the home is the ideal we are aiming at, what concrete measures can bring us closer to making this the social norm supported by public policy as well as popular culture? First, keeping in mind the law of unintended consequences, we can remove the perverse incentives that have discouraged care at home— just as welfare reform has begun to dismantle a system that has fostered a culture of dependency and demoralized an underclass of poor recipients. Ending the direct subsidies provided to commercial center-based child care would seem an obvious starting point. As one analyst for the Department of Health and Human Services has observed,

> [I]f subsidies have increased over the years, then one could hypothesize that the kinds of care more often subsidized— and thus, cheaper to parents—would increase in prevalence. Since center care has traditionally and increasingly been subsidized by both government and perhaps by providers themselves, one would expect an increase in the use of center care compared to the use of relative care. In fact, we do see an increase in the use of center care and a decline in the use of relative care.[11]

We should not forget that the long-range effort to increase the federal role in childrearing, while offered as a "gift" to families in the form of block grants and tax subsidies, must be paid for, in the form of an increased tax burden, by other families.

And it is far from apparent that the path of increased federal involvement in the form of greater regulation of the day care industry is even effective in achieving the limited goal of increased quality of care. More regulation of the industry, particularly on the federal level, would boost the cost of child care and discourage many smaller, family-based providers from doing business. One study showed that simply making the median of the state-mandated minimum staff-to-children ratios a national minimum ratio would put one-third of licensed facilities out of business due to the increased cost.[12] Already, states with stricter standards for staff-to-children ratios have fewer available child care facilities relative to their populations.[13] Even the liberal Brookings Institution has acknowledged that more regulation will "decrease the supply and raise the costs" of care, and "ironically, result in fewer regulated facilities." And staff-to-children ratios are not the only issue; the total costs associated with a regulatory regime determined to enforce "high quality" standards of child care as defined by bureaucrats would be astronomical. Countless unlicensed family day care operations, some of them among the highest quality in terms of stability of care arrangements and individual attention, would be forced to close under such a regime.

If we believe, however, that in-home parental care is highly desirable, then we must go beyond eliminating the penalties imposed on parents by a regime of subsidies to commercial day care. We must acknowledge the sacrifices that parents make to invest in the upbringing of their children, and the central part those sacrifices play in sustaining a vital economy, by compensating those parents. Harvard's Richard Gill has suggested the equivalent of a G.I. Bill of Rights for young parents engaged in raising their own children. Gill recommends allowing "such stay-at-home parents to earn points toward future training—at high school, vocational school, college, professional school, or even post-professional school—when their children reach school age."[14]

Other benefits that are truly family-friendly, allowing employees time at home to fulfill their family obligations rather than insuring their full-time presence in the workplace, are remarkably little utilized by most corporations. While an impressive-sounding 13 million people work from their homes in the United States, fully half of those are running their own independent businesses (many of them consultants), and over 3 million of those have other office jobs. Only about 600,000 are allowed to work from home by their employers.[15] Policies like comp time, flex time, part-time work with benefits, priority scheduling for parents, and telecommuting are all relatively rare in the corporate world compared with investment and subsidies for day care. Even for families with preschoolers in which both parents are working, more flexibility in work schedules would significantly reduce the time that a child had to spend in out-of-home care while not measurably affecting family income. One big barrier to the implementation of more flexible scheduling is antiquated labor law, kept in place through the influence of old-line union officials determined to defend seniority systems and collective bargaining agreements. It may be time to reexamine some of those old positions, particularly in light of the increasing popularity of flexible scheduling options among employees. Businesses might even be offered tax breaks themselves for adopting such policies as telecommuting, flex time and benefits for part-time workers.

But even more important than rewarding corporations with "family-friendly" policies that actually live up to the name is the necessity of restoring the political acknowledgement of married parents' contribution to the economic and social order, particularly as this is embodied in the tax code. In the mid-1950s, about half of all married couples with children were paying essentially no income tax as a result of the personal exemption (worth about $10,000 in today's terms). Raising the current personal exemption of $3,000 significantly would relieve the growing tax burden on families with children, make more possible the option of one parent staying at home to care for the kids, and acknowledge the indispensable social value of the time and effort that parents put into the rearing and formation of their children. Letting parents keep more of their money for being parents leaves the child care decision to them, and chances are they will choose to do it themselves if given the opportunity.

More achievable, perhaps, is universalizing and expanding the current dependent-care tax credit, making it available on a nondiscriminatory basis to all families with young children instead of just those who put their children in commercial day care. This is a fairly easy case to make in political terms: why should we be subsidizing the child care choice that is least popular among parents while providing no equivalent subsidy to the majority that chooses less formal arrangements or cares for their own children at home? If they were made aware of it, most parents would regard the current exclusive incentive for day care as positively perverse family policy. This measure is also perhaps the most effective foil against those commercial day care proponents who claim that concern for children's welfare is evinced only by support for increasing subsidies to commercial care. It takes nothing away from single parents and others who currently depend on commercial child care, while expanding the options for all parents.

Social and taxation policies that allow parents to invest more time and effort in the formation of their children—that value this investment in "human capital"—may be the most effective thing government can do to insure our future economic growth and competitiveness. This is particularly relevant in the debate over child care policy. In former times the federal government's approach to child care was to give families the money (in the form of tax deductions for children) to do what families exist to do—to take care of the children themselves. For the last thirty-five years, however, as the value of the child deduction has steadily shrunk, the feds have made it even tougher for parents at home by providing substantial write-offs for parents who choose commercial day care.

Among the positive changes that could be made, one temptation to avoid in family policy is to follow the European model. A growing contingent of family advocates in the United States suggest that the system of paid maternal leave, universal government-provided child care, and state subsidies for all children regardless of their parents' status is one that the United States would do well to follow. But the European experience appears to be more a cautionary tale than a success story. As Maggie Gallagher has asked, "If Europe is so good at resolving work/family dilemmas, why is the European family disappearing?" The low birthrates of virtually every nation in Europe portend an economic and social crisis of catastrophic dimensions in the coming decades, as fewer and fewer workers are supporting an ever growing system of public pensions. Universal child care, paid maternal leave and indiscriminate child subsidies have all added to the increasingly unsupportable welfare system, increased the tax burden for all families and contributed to the birth dearth. This supposedly family-friendly system actually does nothing to value the contributions that parents make in their homes, outside of the money economy and the competitive labor market, while it maximizes the labor force participation of mothers by sending the message that several months of leave is enough for both mothers and children. When social policy fails to support married mothers' work in the home, one finds that even under a "generous" system of mandated leave and benefits, those mothers will typically have only one child; any more would mean too great a reduction of their labor force commitment to derive any advantage.

WHILE POLICY CHANGES AIMED AT making the economy and the tax code more friendly to families are important, they are not enough. Just as policy changes that worked against the family cannot entirely explain the family decline that began after the end of the baby boom in the mid-1960s, so policy changes favorable to family formation and unity will not entirely remedy the situation. There has always been and will continue to be a large cultural element in private decisions made regarding the family, an element which includes the degree of confidence in the future, religious belief and practice, and the status accorded nonmarket work.

A key element in the cultural battle is the courage necessary to state the truth and get beyond the politically correct posturing that has so distorted the public discussion of child care policy. Keeping children's interests in the forefront of the debate is of the utmost importance in maintaining an attitude of candor. When confronted by an audience stocked with young feminists hostile to her opposition to the regular use of nonparental day care, radio host Dr. Laura Schlessinger asked the crowd one simple question: "If you could ... come back as an infant, stand up if you would rather be raised by a daycare worker, a nanny or a babysitter [rather than your own mother]. Stand up now." Not one of the women in the audience moved. "Then why," she asked, "are you going to do this to your children?"[16]

It's a question that needs to be asked not only of the relatively few parents who prefer day care for their children, but of a day care establishment that would foist the destructive regime of universal day care for preschoolers on every family, all in the name of concern over children's well-being and development.

ACKNOWLEDGMENTS

I would like to thank the trustees of the Charlotte and Walter Kohler Charitable Trust, whose support of the Kohler Fellows program at the Howard Center made this book possible; Allan Carlson, whose scholarship, support and encouragement allowed me to complete this project; Jeane Heise, whose friendship and hospitality made my summer stay in the heartland so enjoyable; and Peter Collier, a real pro whose helpful suggestions and critiques made this a better book.

Notes

Introduction

1. David Gelernter, "Why Mothers Should Stay Home," *Commentary,* February 1996, p. 25.

2. Yvonne Zylan, "Maternalism Redefined: Gender, the State, and the Politics of Day Care, 1945–1962," *Gender and Society* 14:5 (October 2000), pp. 608–29.

3. Ibid.

4. U.S. Census Bureau, *Statistical Abstract of the United States: 2002,* 122nd ed. (Washington, D.C.: U.S. Government Printing Office).

5. Allan C. Carlson, *The Family in America,* March 1998, p. 3.

6. Allan C. Carlson, *Family Questions* (New Brunswick: Transaction Publishers, 1988), p. 9.

7. Ibid.

8. Phyllis Schlafly in *The Politics of Daycare: Who Will Rock the Cradle?* ed. Phyllis Schlafly (Washington, D.C.: Eagle Forum Education and Legal Defense Fund, 1989), p. 249.

9. Ibid., p. 250.

10. Ibid., p. 249.

11. Carlson, *The Family in America;* Deborah Fallows, *A Mother's Work* (Boston: Houghton Mifflin, 1985), p. 176.

12. Allan C. Carlson, *From Cottage to Work Station: The Family's Search for Social Harmony in the Industrial Age* (San Francisco: Ignatius Press, 1993), p. 23.

13. William R. Mattox Jr., "Men at Work: Crafting Employment Policies to Facilitate Fathering," *Insight,* June 1993, p. 3.

14. Ronald Reagan, *Public Papers of the Presidents of the United States, 1988–89,* Book II, *July 2, 1988, to January 19, 1989* (Washington, D.C.: U.S. Government Printing Office, 1991).

15. Dana Mack, *The Assault on Parenthood: How Our Culture Undermines the Family* (New York: Simon & Schuster, 1997), p. 176.

16. Ibid., p. 177.

17. Ibid., p. 178.

18. Ibid., p. 180.

19. 2000 Green Book: Background Material and Data on Programs within the Jurisdiction of the Committee on Ways and Means, Committee on Ways and Means, U.S. House of Representatives (Washington, D.C.: U.S. Government Printing Office, 2001).

20. B. Fuller and S. L. Kagan, *Remember the Children: Mothers Balance Work and Child Care under Welfare Reform,* Wave 1 Report, Growing Up in Poverty Project 2000 (Berkeley: University of California, 2000).

21. Mack, *The Assault on Parenthood,* p. 181.

22. 2000 Green Book.

23. Lance Gay, "Outrageous Frauds in Federal Day Care," *Scripps Howard News Service,* 27 September 2000.

24. 1996 Green Book: Background Material and Data on Programs within the Jurisdiction of the Committee on Ways and

Means, Committee on Ways and Means, U.S. House of Representatives (Washington, D.C.: U.S. Government Printing Office,
1996); Heidi L. Brennan, "White House Child Care Conference,"
Welcome Home, December 1997.

25. Charles Siegel, *What's Wrong with Day Care* (New York:
Teachers' College Press, 2001), p. 13.

One: A Lethal Reticence

1. Misty Bernall, *She Said Yes: The Unlikely Martyrdom of Cassie
Bernall* (New York: Pocket Books, 1999), pp. 43–81.

2. Harry Rosenfeld, "Seeking the Answer to the Unanswerable," *Albany Times Union,* 25 April 1999, p. B5; Jim Nolan and
April Adamson, "Are We at Fault As a Nation?" *Philadelphia Daily
News,* 28 April 1999, p. 6; Jordana Willner, "Kids Turn So Violent
and High School Is So Hellish—Why?" *San Francisco Chronicle,*
28 April 1999, p. A21.

3. Leonard Pitts, "Family, All Together All Alone," *Denver
Post,* 28 November 1999, p. G3. Key findings from this study can
be found at:
www.kff.org/content/1999/1535/pressreleasefinal.doc.html.

4. Judith Shulevitz, "I Want My Electronic Baby Sitter!" *Slate*
(www.slate.com), 5 August 1999.

5. Donna Britt, "Our Children Going Down with the Tube,"
Washington Post, 19 November 1999, p. B1.

6. NBC/*Wall Street Journal* polls, conducted by the Roper Center at the University of Connecticut, 16–19 June and 24–26 July
1999, released August 1999.

7. Ann Scales, "Clinton Vows to Let States Help Parents,"
Boston Globe, 24 May 1999.

8. Michael Janofsky, "Columbine Panel Blames Lack of Action for Deaths," *New York Times,* 17 May 2001, p. A12; Eric Pooley, "Portrait of a Deadly Bond," *Time,* 10 May 1999, p. 26.

9. Allan Prendergast, "Doom Rules," *Denver Westword,* 5 August 1999, Features section.

10. Dave Cullen, "Goodbye Cruel World," *Salon,* 14 December 1999.

11. Ellen Goodman, "Blame the Parents? It's Easy—and Wrong," *Boston Globe,* 2 May 1999, p. E7.

12. Dale Russakoff, Amy Goldstein and Joel Achenbach, "In Littleton, Neighbors Ponder What Went Wrong," *Washington Post,* 2 May 1999, p. A1.

13. Mary Eberstadt, "Home Alone America," *Policy Review,* no. 107, June 2001 (www.policyreview.org/JUN01/eberstadt.html).

14. William Damon, *Greater Expectations* (New York: Diane Publishing Co., 1999).

15. Centers for Disease Control and Prevention, "Rates of Homicide, Suicide, and Firearm-Related Death among Children—26 Industrialized Countries," *Morbidity and Mortality Weekly Report,* 7 February 1997.

16. Robert D. Putnam, *Bowling Alone* (New York: Touchstone, 2001), using data from U.S. Public Health Service and other sources.

17. Jacqueline F. de Gaston, Larry Jensen and Stan Weed, "A Closer Look at Adolescent Sexual Activity," *Journal of Youth and Adolescence* 24 (1995), pp. 465–78.

18. Alan Guttmacher Institute, *Sex and America's Teenagers* (New York: Guttmacher Institute, 1994), pp. 19, 24; Joyce C. Abma and Freya L. Sonenstein, *Sexual Activity and Contraceptive*

Practices among Teenagers in the United States, 1988 and 1995,
Series 23: Data from the National Survey of Family Growth,
National Center for Health Statistics, Washington, D.C., April
2001, Table 1.

19. Kay Hymowitz, "What's Wrong with the Kids?" *City Journal,* Winter 2000, pp. 40–48.

20. Sylvia Ann Hewlett and Cornel West, *The War against Parents* (Boston: Houghton Mifflin, 1998), p. 79.

21. Elizabeth M. Aldeman and Stanford B. Friedman, "Behavioral Problems of Affluent Youth," *Pediatric Annals* 24 (1994), pp. 186–91.

22. Mark Warr, "Parents, Peers, and Delinquency," *Social Forces* 72 (1993), pp. 247–64.

23. Eberstadt, "Home Alone America."

24. Joel Paris and Hallie Frank, "Perceptions of Parental Bonding in Borderline Patients," *American Journal of Psychiatry* 146 (1989), pp. 1498–99.

25. Children's Defense Fund, *The State of America's Children Yearbook* (Washington, D.C.: Children's Defense Fund, 1995).

26. Patrick Fagan, "The Child Abuse Crisis: The Disintegration of Marriage, Family, and the American Community," Heritage Foundation Backgrounder, no. 1:115, 3 June 1997.

27. Eberstadt, "Home Alone America."

28. Sarah Crane, "Adolescents, Time after School: Solitude and Its Implications," M.A. Thesis, University of Chicago, August 1999.

29. Richard T. Gill, *Posterity Lost: Progress, Ideology, and the Decline of the American Family* (Lanham, Md.: Rowman & Littlefield Publishers, 1997), p. 31.

30. Cited in Eberstadt, "Home Alone America."

31. Dr. T. Berry Brazelton on ABC's *Oprah Winfrey Show,* 16 May 1995.

32. Penelope Leach, *Children First: What Our Society Must Do and Is Not Doing for Our Children* (New York: Alfred Knopf, 1994), p. 206.

33. "What Mothers Want Today and Every Day; Actually, Both Men and Women Would Like More Family Time," *Los Angeles Times,* 14 May 1995, p. M4.

34. *Los Angeles Times* poll, 25 April–1 May 1999.

35. Ellen Galinsky et al., "The Changing Workforce: Highlights of the National Study," Families and Work Institute, New York, 1993.

36. Barbara Vobejda, "Love Conquers What Ails Teens, Study Finds," *Washington Post,* 10 September 1997, p. A1.

37. Cal Thomas, "Kids Are Tuned In to Reality," *Dayton Daily News,* 3 March 1995, p. A11.

38. Peter L. Benson, *The Troubled Journey: A Portrait of 6th–12th Grade Youth* (Minneapolis: Search Institute, 1993), p. 84.

39. Ellen Galinsky, *Ask the Children: What America's Children Really Think about Working Parents* (New York: William Morrow & Co., 1999).

40. William R. Mattox, "America's Family Time Famine," *Children Today,* November/December 1990. Seven years after Mattox's original analysis, Robinson publicly claimed that Mattox's use of his statistics was "uninformed," since it was based on Robinson's own purported "miscalculations" and computer-generated errors in his original study. Despite the fact that he produced no evidence to show that any of this was the case,

Robinson's "confession" was featured in a *U.S. News and World Report* story claiming that the "parental time deficit" was a myth.

41. "Got the Time?" *Economist,* 26 June 1999.

42. Laura Potts, "Children Spending More Time with Parents Than Twenty Years Ago," Associated Press.

43. "Media and Day Care," www.geocities.com/Wellesley/Garden/2010/media.html.

44. Mary Eberstadt, book review in *Commentary,* 1 November 1999, p. 55.

45. Stanley I. Greenspan, M.D., *The Four-Thirds Solution: Solving the Child-Care Crisis in America Today* (Cambridge, Mass.: Perseus Publishing, 2000), p. 5.

46. Isabelle Fox and Norman M. Lobsenz, *Being There: The Benefits of a Stay-at-Home Parent,* Barrons Educational Series (Hauppauge, New York, 1996), p. 63.

47. Kristin Smith, *Who's Minding the Kids? Child Care Arrangements: Spring 1997,* U.S. Census Bureau, Current Population Reports, July 2002, Table 1, p. 3.

48. National Center for Education Statistics, "Characteristics of Children's Early Care and Education Programs," June 1998. Data from Sandra L. Hofferth, Kimberlee A. Shauman, Robert Henke and Jerry West, "National Household Educational Survey, 1995," NCES Publication 989-128 (Washington, D.C.: NCES, 1998).

48. Smith, *Who's Minding the Kids? Child Care Arrangements: Spring 1997,* Table 1, p. 3; Table 3, p. 8.

50. Bettye M. Caldwell, "Infant Day Care—The Outcast Gains Respectability" in Pamela Roby, ed., *Child Care—Who Cares: Foreign and Domestic Infant and Early Childhood Development Policies* (New York: Basic Books, 1973), p. 21.

51. Charles Siegel, *What's Wrong with Day Care* (New York: Teachers' College Press, 2001), p. 47; U.S. Census Bureau, *Statistical Abstract of the United States: 2001,* No. 557, p. 359.

52. *Statistical Abstract of the United States: 2001,* No. 554, p. 358; Smith, *Who's Minding the Kids? Child Care Arrangements: Spring 1997,* Table 1, p. 3.

53. *Who's Minding the Kids? Child Care Arrangements: Fall 1995,* Table 2, p. 5.

54. Ibid., Figure 1, p. 5.

55. NICHD Early Childhood Research Network, "Quality Child Care and Child Development Prior to School," paper presented by Deborah Low Vandell at the meeting of the Society for Research in Child Development, Minneapolis, 19–22 April 2001. "Child Care and Mother Care Interaction in the First Three Years of Life," *Developmental Psychology* 35 (1999), pp. 1399–1413. "The Effects of Infant Child Care on Infant-Mother Attachment Security," *Child Development* 68:5 (September/October 1997), pp. 860–79. D. L. Vandell and M. A. Corsanti, "Variations in Early Child Care: Do They Predict Subsequent Social, Emotional and Cognitive Differences?" *Early Childhood Research Quarterly,* 1990.

56. S. Helburn et al., "Cost, Quality and Child Outcomes Study," public report, University of Colorado-Denver, Department of Economics, 1995. NICHD Early Child Care Research Network, "Characteristics and Quality of Childcare for Toddlers and Preschoolers," *Applied Developmental Science* 4(3), pp. 116–35.

57. Greenspan, *The Four-Thirds Solution,* p. 41.

58. National Center of Education Statistics, U.S. Department of Education, "Characteristics of Children's Early Care and Education Programs, 1995."

59. The NICHD Early Childhood Care Research Network, "Child Care in the First Year of Life," *Merrill-Palmer Quarterly* 43 (1997), pp. 340–60.

60. Bernard Goldberg, *Bias: A CBS Insider Exposes How the Media Distort the News* (Washington, D.C.: Regnery Publishing), pp. 163–78.

Two: An Intolerable Truth

1. Sheryl Gay Stolberg, "Public Lives: Another Academic Salvo in the Nation's 'Mommy Wars,'" *New York Times,* 21 April 2001, p. A8.

2. Kay S. Hymowitz, "Fear and Loathing at the Day-Care Center," *City Journal* 11:3 (Summer 2001).

3. Remarks by Jay Belsky at a consultation on "The Risks of Day Care," sponsored by The Rockford Institute in Chicago, Illinois, 6 December 1988.

4. Elizabeth Harvey, "Short-Term and Long-Term Effects of Early Parental Employment on Children of the National Longitudinal Survey of Youth," *Developmental Psychology,* March 1999, pp. 445–59.

5. "Good News for Moms: No One Misses You," *Vital STATS: The Numbers Behind the News,* Newsletter of the Statistical Assessment Service, March 1999, p. 1.

6. Barbara Vobejda, "Mothers' Employment Works for Children: Study Finds No Long-Term Damage," *Washington Post,* 1 March 1999, p. A1.

7. Paul Recer, "Working Moms Not Shortchanging Kids, Study Suggests," *Atlanta Journal and Constitution,* 1 March 1999, p. A1.

8. Paul Recer, "Keep Your Day Job, Mom: Study Suggests Kids Will Be Fine," *Newark Star-Ledger,* 1 March 1999, p. 21.

9. Diane Fisher, "When Science Serves Politics," *Investor's Business Daily,* 5 March 1999, Viewpoint.

10. Recer, "Working Moms Not Shortchanging Kids."

11. "Good News for Moms," *Vital STATS,* p. 1.

12. Ibid.

13. Tom Zoellner, "Day Care: Study on Putting Your Kids in Day Care," *Men's Health,* 1 September 1999.

14. Ibid. and "Good News for Moms," *Vital STATS.*

15. "New Longitudinal Study Finds That Having a Working Mother Does No Significant Harm to Children," American Psychological Association press release, 18 February 1999.

16. Zoellner, "Day Care."

17. Shankar Vedantam, "Child Aggressiveness Study Cites Day Care," *Washington Post,* 19 April 2001, p. A6.

18. Ibid.

19. Panel debate, "Does Daycare Create Aggressive Kids?" *Talkback Live 15:00,* CNN, 23 April 2001.

20. Editorial, *Philadelphia Inquirer,* 28 April 2001, p. A8.

21. Nancy Gibbs, "What Kids (Really) Need," *Time,* 30 April 2001, p. 48.

22. Meghan Mutchler Deerin, "Shedding Light on the Day-Care Doom and Gloom," *Chicago Tribune,* 15 July 2001, Health & Family, p. 1.

23. Ibid.

24. Valerie Strauss, "Child Care Worries Adding Up," *Washington Post,* 30 April 2001, p. A1.

25. Marilyn Gardner, "Media's Eye on Moms," *Christian Science Monitor,* 30 May 2001, p. 12.

26. Catherine Arnst, "Relax, Mom. Day Care Won't Ruin the Kids," *Business Week Online* (www.businessweek.com), 7 May 2001, News: Analysis & Commentary.

27. Panel debate, "Does Daycare Create Aggressive Kids?"

28. Ibid.

29. Deerin, "Shedding Light on the Day-Care Doom and Gloom."

30. Ibid.

31. Jay Belsky, "Childcare McCarthyism," *National Review Online,* Guest Comment, 9 May 2001.

32. Deerin, "Shedding Light on the Day-Care Doom and Gloom."

33. Ibid.

34. Gardner, "Media's Eye on Moms."

35. Strauss, "Child Care Worries Adding Up."

36. Panel debate, "Does Daycare Create Aggressive Kids?"

37. Jennifer Foote Sweeney, "The Day-Care Scare, Again," *Salon.com,* 21 April 2001.

38. Peggy Orenstein, "Bringing Down Baby," *Los Angeles Times,* 29 April 2001, p. M1.

39. Cathy Young, "New Squabble over Day Care," *Boston Globe,* 25 April 2001, p. A27.

40. Jessica Garrison, "Researchers in Child-Care Study Claim Study Has Been Misrepresented," *Los Angeles Times,* 26 April 2001.

41. Carol Guensburg, "Bully Factories?" *American Journalism Review,* July/August 2001.

42. Arnst, "Relax, Mom. Day Care Won't Ruin the Kids."

43. Guensburg, "Bully Factories?"

44. Jennifer Foote Sweeney, "Jay Belsky Doesn't Play Well with Others," *Salon.com,* 26 April 2001.

45. Maggie Gallagher, "Day Careless," *National Review,* 26 January 1998.

46. Ibid.

47. Garrison, "Researchers in Child-Care Study Claim Study Has Been Misrepresented."

48. Lynn Smith, "Putting a Spin on the Truth with Statistics and Studies," *Los Angeles Times,* 6 June 2001, Section 5, p. 1.

49. Zoellner, "Day Care."

50. Gallagher, "Day Careless."

51. Strauss, "Child Care Worries Adding Up."

52. Gardner, "Media's Eye on Moms."

53. Ibid.

54. Ibid.

55. Ibid.

56. Ibid.

57. Ibid.

58. Ibid.

59. Smith, "Putting a Spin on the Truth."

Three: A Conspiracy of Silence

1. Maggie Gallagher, "Day Careless," *National Review,* 26 January 1998.

2. Karl Zinsmeister, "Longstanding Warnings from Experts," *American Enterprise,* May/June 1998, pp. 34–35.

3. Karl Zinsmeister, "Why Encouraging Day Care Is Unwise," *American Enterprise,* May/June 1998, pp. 4–7.

4. Ibid.

5. Ibid.

6. John Bowlby, *A Secure Base: Parent-Child Attachment and Healthy Human Development* (New York: Basic Books, 1988).

7. Bryce Christensen, ed., *Day Care: Child Psychology and Adult Economics* (Rockford, Illinois: Rockford Institute, 1989), p. vii.

8. William D. Gairdner, *The War against the Family* (Toronto: Stoddart Publishing, 1992), p. 340.

9. Ibid.

10. M. Erickson, L. A. Sroufe and B. Egeland, *The Relationship between Quality of Attachment and Behavior Problems in Preschool in a High Risk Sample* (Monographs for the Society for Research in Child Development, 1985), pp. 162, 149.

11. Ken Magid and Carole McKelvey, *High Risk: Children without a Conscience* (New York: Bantam Books, 1988), p. 4.

12. Ibid.

13. Margaret Talbot, "Attachment Theory: The Ultimate Experiment," *New York Times Magazine,* 24 May 1998, pp. 27–30.

14. Marian Blum, *The Day-Care Dilemma: Women and Children First* (Lexington: Lexington Books, 1983), pp. 92–93.

15. Ibid.

16. Ibid.

17. Ibid.

18. Karl Zinsmeister, "The Problem with Day Care," *American Enterprise,* May/June 1998, pp. 33–36.

19. Ibid.

20. Christopher Lasch, *Haven in a Heartless World: The Family Besieged* (New York: Basic Books, 1978), p. 8.

21. Mary Eberstadt, "Putting Children Last," *Commentary*, October 1995, p. 44.

22. *San Francisco Chronicle*, 3 May 1990, p. B4.

23. Eberstadt, "Putting Children Last."

24. Ibid.

25. Maggie Gallagher, *Enemies of Eros* (Washington, D.C.: Regnery, 1996), p. 78.

26. Peter Barglow et al., "Effects of Maternal Absence Due to Employment on the Quality of Infant-Mother Attachment in a Low-Risk Sample," *Child Development* 58 (August 1987).

27. Jay Belsky, "Infant Day Care and Socioemotional Development: The United States," *Journal of Child Psychology and Psychiatry* 29:4 (1988), pp. 397–406.

28. Carolee Howes and Claire E. Hamilton, "Children's Relationships with Caregivers: Mothers and Child Care Teachers," *Child Development* 63 (1992), pp. 859–66.

29. Gallagher, "Day Careless."

30. Virginia L. Colin, *Human Attachment: What We Know Now*, Literature Review on Infant Attachment prepared under contract for the Office of the Assistant Secretary for Planning and Evaluation, Department of Health and Human Services, 18 June 1991, pp. 20–22; Charmaine Crouse Yoest, "Behind the Push for Day Care," *Family Policy*, March 1998.

31. Mohammadreza Hojat, "Satisfaction with Early Relationships with Parents and Psychosocial Attributes in Adulthood: Which Parent Contributes More?" *Journal of Genetic Psychology* 159 (1998), pp. 203–20.

32. Zinsmeister, "Longstanding Warnings from Experts."

33. Robert Karen, *Becoming Attached* (New York: Warner Books, 1994), pp. 5–6, 13, 249, 323–40, 392.

34. Stanley I. Greenspan, M.D., *The Four-Thirds Solution: Solving the Child-Care Crisis in America Today* (Cambridge, Massachusetts: Perseus Publishing, 2001), pp. 49–50.

35. Penelope Leach, *Children First: What Our Society Must Do and Is Not Doing for Our Children* (New York: Alfred Knopf, 1994), p. 92.

36. University of North Carolina–Frances Parker Study reported by R. Haskins, "Public School Aggression amongst Children with Varying Day-Care Experience," *Child Development* 56, pp. 689–703; Jay Belsky, "Infant Day Care: A Cause for Concern," *Zero to Three* (special reprint of article, September 1986), p. 6.

37. Deborah L. Vandell and Mary A. Corasanti, "Variations in Early Child Care: Do They Predict Subsequent Social, Emotional, and Cognitive Differences?" *Early Childhood Research Quarterly*, 1990.

38. Kathy Tout et al., "Social Behavior Correlates of Cortisol Activity in Child Care: Gender Differences and Time-of-Day Effects," *Child Development* 69 (1998), pp. 1247–62.

39. Jerome Kagan, Richard Kearsley and Philip Zelazo, *Infancy: Its Place in Human Development,* quoted in Dana Mack, *The Assault on Parenthood: How Our Culture Undermines the Family* ((New York: Simon & Schuster, 1997), p. 171.

40. Kay S. Hymowitz, "Fear and Loathing at the Day-Care Center," *City Journal* 11:3 (Summer 2001).

41. Gallagher, "Day Careless."

42. Leach, *Children First,* p. 92.

43. Lisabeth F. DiLalla, "Daycare Child, and Family Influences on Preschoolers' Social Behaviors in a Peer Setting," *Child Study Journal* 28:3 (1998), pp. 223–44.

44. Arminta Jacobson and Susan Owen, "Infant-Caregiver Interactions in Day Care," *Child Study Journal* 17 (1987), pp. 197–209.

45. www.fpg.unc.edu/~abc.

46. John T. Bruer, *The Myth of the First Three Years* (New York: Free Press, 1999), p. 91.

47. Christopher Jencks et al., *Inequality: A Reassessment of the Effect of Family and Schooling in America* (New York: Basic Books, 1972), pp. 158–59.

48. Lawrence Steinberg, *Beyond the Classroom: Why School Reform Has Failed and What Parents Need to Do* (New York: Simon & Schuster, 1996), pp. 118–99.

49. Gallagher, "Day Careless."

50. From "Attachment Disorder: What the Experts Say," www.jbaassoc.demon.co.uk/kate/attachmentexpert.htm.

51. Ibid.

52. Vandell and Corasanti, "Variations in Early Child Care."

53. From www.geocities.com./Wellesley/Garden/2010/day-carestats. html, p. 2.

54. Kathy Sylva, "School Influences on Children's Development," *Journal of Child Psychology and Psychiatry* 35:1 (1994), pp. 135–70.

55. Robert A. Hoekelman, "Day Care, Day Care: Mayday! Mayday!" *Pediatric Annals* 20 (1991), p. 403.

56. Cynthia G. Olsen, Carmen P. Wong, Richard E. Gordon, David J. Harper and Philip S. Whitecar, "The Role of the Family Physician in the Day Care Setting," *American Family Physician,* 15 September 1996.

57. Memphis State University study and *American Journal of Public Health* article cited in Karl Zinsmeister "The Problem with Day Care," *American Enterprise,* May/June 1998, p. 41.

58. David M. Bell, "Illness Associated with Child Day Care: A Study of Incidence and Cost," *American Journal of Public Health* 79 (1989), pp. 479–84.

59. John L. Ey et al., "Passive Smoke Exposure and Otitis Media in the First Year of Life," *Pediatrics* 95 (1995), pp. 670–77; Pekka L. Louhiala et al., "Form of Day Care and Respiratory Infections among Finnish Children," *American Journal of Public Health* 85 (1995), pp. 1109–12.

60. Harriet B. Presser, "Place of Child Care and Medicated Respiratory Illness among Young American Children," *Journal of Marriage and the Family* 50 (1988), pp. 2581–84.

61. See reference to 1995 study in *Pediatric Infectious Disease Journal* in Carol Potera, "Look, Ma! No Pneumococcus!" *Environmental Health Perspectives,* June 1999, pp. A312–13.

62. Stephen R. Redmond and Michael E Pichichero, "Hemophilus Influenza Type B Disease: An Epidemiologic Study with Special Reference to Day Care Centers," *Journal of the American Medical Association* 252 (1984), pp. 2581–84; Robert E. Black, "Giardiasis in Day Care Centers: Evidence of Person-to-Person Transmission," *Pediatrics* 60 (1977), pp. 486–89.

63. Olsen et al., "Role of the Family Physician."

64. Ibid.

65. See Georges Peter et al., eds., *Report of the Committee on Infectious Diseases* (Elk Grove: American Academy of Pediatrics, 1986), pp. 54–58; Stephen C. Hadler et al., "Hepatitis A in Day Care Centers," *New England Journal of Medicine* 302 (1980), pp. 1222–27.

65. Rachel Y. Moon et al., "Sudden Infant Death Syndrome in Child Care Settings," *Pediatrics* 106 (2000), pp. 295–300.

67. See David M. Bell, "Illness Associated with Child Day Care: A Study of Incidence and Cost," *American Journal of Public Health* 79 (1989), pp. 479–83; Lynne Vernon-Feagans, Elizabeth E. Manlove and Brenda L. Volling, "Otitis Media and the Social Behavior of Children," *Child Development* 67 (1996), pp. 1528–39.

68. See Jody R. Murphy et al., "Epidemiology of Congenital Cytomegalovirus Infection: Maternal Risk Factors and Molecular Analysis of Cytomegalovirus Strains," *American Journal of Epidemiology* 147 (1988), pp. 940–47.

69. Josette Raymond et al., "Sequential Colonization by *Streptococcus Pneumoniae* of Healthy Children Living in an Orphanage," *Journal of Infectious Diseases* 181 (2000), pp. 1983–88.

70. Stanley H. Schuman, "Day Care Associated Infection: More Than Meets the Eye," *Journal of the American Medical Association* 249 (1983), p. 76.

71. *Health,* October 1991.

72. Schuman, "Day Care Associated Infection."

73. Gairdner, *The War against the Family,* p. 342.

74. See Howard Bauchner et al., "Improving Parent Knowledge about Antibiotics: A Video Intervention," *Pediatrics* 108 (2001), pp. 845–50.

75. Howard Bauchner, Stephen Pelton and Jerome O. Klein, "Parents, Physicians, and Antibiotic Use," *Pediatrics* 103 (1999), pp. 395–401.

76. Ibid.

77. Louise S. Barden et al., "Current Attitudes Regarding Use of Antimicrobial Agents: Results from Physicians' and Parents' Focus Group Discussions," *Clinical Pediatrics* 37 (1998), pp. 665–71.

78. James D. Kellner et al., "*Streptococcus pneumoniae* Carriage in Children Attending 59 Canadian Child Care Centers," *Archives of Pediatric and Adolescent Medicine* 153 (1999), pp. 495–502.

79. "Levels of Inappropriate Antibiotic Prescriptions Significantly Reduced with Community-Wide Education," *Pediatrics* 108 (2001), pp. 575–83.

80. See Richard Saltus, "Return of the Germ," *American Health*, September 1994, p. 72.

81. Ibid.

82. A. S. Ryan, "The Resurgence of Breastfeeding in the United States," *Pediatrics* 99:4 (1997), p. e12.

83. American Academy of Pediatrics, "Breastfeeding and the Use of Human Milk," *Pediatrics* 100:6 (1997), pp. 1035–39.

84. Richard Morin, "Unconventional Wisdom," *Washington Post*, 1 October 2000, p. B5.

Four: The Day Care Establishment

1. Deborah Fallows, *A Mother's Work* (Boston: Houghton Mifflin, 1985), pp. 71–72.

2. Ibid, pp. 189–91.

3. Ellen Goodman, "It's Not as Bad as It Seems for the Brat Pack," *Boston Globe*, 26 April 2001.

4. Robert Karen, *Becoming Attached* (New York: Warner Books, 1994), p. 346.

5. Ann Crittenden, *The Price of Motherhood*, cited in Kay Hymowitz, "Fear and Loathing at the Day-Care Center," *City Journal* 11:3 (Summer 2001).

6. Sherri Eisenberg, "When It Comes to Day Care, You Can't Trust the Media," *Washington Monthly*, June 1997, p. 15.

7. Tom Zoellner, "Day Care: Study on Putting Your Kids in Day Care," *Men's Health*, 1 September 1999.

8. Susan Chira, *A Mother's Place: Choosing Work and Family without Guilt or Blame* (New York: Harper Collins, 1999).

9. Zoellner, "Day Care."

10. Kirstin Downey Grimsley and Jacqueline L. Salmon, "For Working Parents, Mixed News at Home," *Washington Post*, 27 September 1999, p. A1.

11. Ellen Galinsky and William H. Hooks, *The New Extended Family* (Boston: Houghton Mifflin, 1977), p. 248.

12. Zinsmeister, "The Problem with Day Care," *American Enterprise*, May/June 1998, pp. 34–35.

13. Ibid.

14. Stanley I. Greenspen, M.D., *The Four-Thirds Solution: Solving the Childcare Crisis in America Today* (Cambridge, Massachusetts: Perseus Publishing, 2001), p. 38.

15. Zinsmeister, "The Problem with Day Care."

16. Remarks by Jay Belsky at a consultation on "The Risks of Day Care," sponsored by the Rockford Institute in Chicago, Illinois, 6 December 1988.

17. Robert Karen, *Becoming Attached: Unfolding the Mystery of the Infant-Mother Bond and Its Impact on Later Life* (New York: Warner Books, 1994), p. 331; Jay Belsky and David Eggebeen, "Early and Extensive Maternal Employment and Young Children's Socioemotional Development: Children of the National Longitudinal Survey of Youth," *Journal of Marriage and the Family* 53 (1991), pp. 1083–10.

18. Mohammadreza Hojat, "Developmental Pathways to Violence: A Psychodynamic Paradigm," *Peace Psychology Review* 1:2 (Autumn/Winter 1994–95), pp. 176–95.

19. Interview with Mohammadreza Hojat, Ph.D., in *The Family in America* 8:12 (December 1993).

20. L. B. Silverstein, "Transforming the Debate about Child Care and Maternal Employment," *American Psychologist* 46 (1991), pp. 1025–32.

21. Ibid.

22. Mohammadreza Hojat, "Abandoning Research on Consequences of Nonmaternal Care: A Disservice to the Science," *Journal of Social Behavior and Personality* 8 (1993), pp. 5–8.

23. Hymowitz, "Fear and Loathing."

24. Karen, *Becoming Attached,* p. 336.

25. Ibid., p. 334.

26. David Blankenhorn, "Plan B (cont.)," *Propositions,* a publication of the Institute for American Values, no. 12 (Fall 2001).

27. Karen, *Becoming Attached,* p. 320.

28. Ibid.

29. Sandra Scarr, "Mother's Proper Place: Children's Needs and Women's Rights," *Journal of Social Behavior and Personality* 5:6 (November 1990), p. 513.

30. Karen, *Becoming Attached.*

31. Ibid., p. 334.

32. Ibid., p. 332.

33. Zoellner, "Day Care."

34. Sandra Scarr, "Research on Day Care Should Spur a New Look at Old Ideas," *Brown University Child and Adolescent Behavior Letter* 13:12 (December 1997).

35. Jesse Bernard, *The Future of Marriage* (New Haven: Yale University Press, 1982), p. 128.

36. James P. Mitchell in National Manpower Council, *Work in the Lives of Married Women,* pp. 15–19.

37. Brian Robertson, "A Baby's Place Is in the Home," *Human Life Review,* Fall 1990, p. 57.

38. Penelope Leach, *Children First: What Our Society Must Do and Is Not Doing for Our Children* (New York: Alfred Knopf, 1994), p. 79.

39. Dana E. Friedman, "Employer-Supported Child Care: From Benefit to Business Strategy," *Child Care ActioNews* 14:4 (Child Care Action Campaign, July/August 1997).

40. Ibid.

41. Norie Quintos Danyliw, "Got Mother's Milk?" *U.S. News and World Report,* 15 December 1997, p. 79.

42. David Wagner, "Turning Hearts Towards the Office," *Insight,* 22 July 1996, p. 2.

43. Dana Mack, *The Assault on Parenthood: How Our Culture Undermines the Family* ((New York: Simon & Schuster, 1997), p. 190.

44. Randall Wong, "American Business Collaboration Leads Corporate Support," *Child Care Bulletin* 6 (November/December 1995).

45. Richard T. Gill, "Day Care or Parental Care?" *Policy Review,* Spring 1991.

46. Allan Carlson, "The Trojan Horse of Child Care," *Vital Speeches,* 15 April 1998, p. 396.

47. Marian Blum, *The Day-Care Dilemma: Women and Children First* (Lexington: Lexington Books, 1983), p. 96.

48. Ibid., p. 97.

49. Mary Ann Kuharski, "Should We Be Sponsoring Day Care?" *Fidelity,* September 1987, p. 16.

50. Deborah A. Phillips and Carolee Howes, *Quality in Child Care Research* (Washington, D.C.: Research Monographs of the National Association for the Education of Young Children, 1987), vol. 1, p. 1.

51. J. Craig Peery, "Children at Risk: The Case against Day Care," *The Family in America* 5:2 (February 1991).

52. Fallows, *A Mother's Work,* p. 191.

53. Virginia Council on Child Day Care and Early Childhood Programs, "Improper Special Interest Influence in Key Contracts: An Analysis with Preliminary Observations on the Politicized Agenda in Child Day Care," June 1996.

54. Fallows, *A Mother's Work,* p. 166.

55. Ibid., p. 168.

56. Robert Rector, "Myths about Families and Child Care," *Harvard Journal on Legislation* 26:517, pp. 533–34.

57. "Whose Hand Should Rock the Cradle? Child Care for the 21st Century," *CWA Library*, 20 May 1998.

58. Leach, *Children First*, p. 74.

59. Ibid., p. 530.

Five: Working Parents' Necessity or Yuppie Subsidy?

1. U.S. National Center for Education Statistics, *Statistics in Brief*, October 1995 (NCES 95-824).

2. Bureau of the Census, *Current Population Survey P-60* (Washington, D.C., 1996).

3. Frank D. Roylance, "Stay-at-Home Moms Becoming Rarer," www.sunspot.net, 24 October 2000.

4. Lara B. Herscovitch, "Child Care Choices: Low Income Mothers in Bridgeport, Connecticut," *Child and Youth Care Forum* 25:3 (June 1996), pp. 139–52.

5. John L. Kramer, Thomas R. Pope and Lawrence C. Phillips, *Federal Taxation: 1997* (Upper Saddle River, N.J.: Prentice Hall, 1996), pp. 14–15; Estimate by the Urban Institute, cited in the *San Francisco Chronicle*, 8 February 1989, p. C5.

6. Estimate by the Urban Institute, cited in the *San Francisco Chronicle*, 8 February 1989, p. C5.

7. Peggy Noonan, "Looking Forward: What Really Makes Kids Happy," *Good Housekeeping*, January 1998, p. 160.

8. Charles Siegel, *What's Wrong with Day Care* (New York: Teachers' College Press, 2001), p. 9.

9. One study showed that for 5 percent of families, child care expenses exceeded the amount of money earned by the mother even *before* other expenses of working were factored in. April

Brayfield and Sandra L. Hofferth, "Balancing the Family Budget: Differences in Child Care Expenditures by Race, Ethnicity, Economic Status, and Family Structure," *Social Science Quarterly* 76 (1995), pp. 158–77.

10. Summer Harlow, "USDA Study: Average Cost of Raising a Child Is about $165,630," *Kansas City Star,* 12 June 2001.

11. U.S. Bureau of the Census data (median incomes of married-couple families where parents work full-time).

12. Bureau of the Census, Current Population Survey.

13. Lynn White and Stacy J. Rogers, "Economic Circumstances and Family Outcomes: A Review of the 1990s," *Journal of Marriage and the Family* 62 (2000), pp. 1035–51.

14. Lester C. Thurow, "What Boom? Two-thirds of U.S.A. Stuck in 1973," *USA Today,* 11 November 1998.

15. Allan Carlson, *From Cottage to Work Station* (San Francisco: Ignatius Press, 1993), p. 84.

16. Ibid.

17. Diana Furchtgott-Roth, "Working Wives Widen 'Income Gap,'" *Wall Street Journal,* 20 June 1995, p. A18.

18. "Necessary Compromises: How Parents, Employers and Children's Advocates View Child Care Today," *Public Agenda,* August 2000.

19. Ibid.

20. Ibid.

21. See also 1989 Public Opinion survey showing 84 percent of all employed mothers agreeing with the statement, "If I could afford it, I would rather be at home with my children"; 1990 *USA Today* finding that 73 percent of all two-parent families would have one parent stay home with children "if money were not an

issue"; 1994 Labor Department survey showing that while 79 percent of working women liked their jobs, only 15 percent said they would continue to work full-time if they could afford not to; 1996 Wirthlin poll conducted for Concerned Women for America which showed that 80 percent of women would stay home full-time with their children if finances were not a concern; 1997 *Glamour* poll showing that 84 percent of employed women agreed with the statement, "If I could afford it, I would rather be at home with my children," cited in Darcy Olsen, "The Fabricated Crisis in Child Care," Cato Institute Paper, 27 November 1997, p. 2; 1997 Roper poll showing that 75 percent of Americans believe that mothers who work outside the home and have children under the age of three "threaten family values," cited in the *Wall Street Journal,* 8 January 1998, editorial page.

22. "The Parent Trap," *Parents,* March 2000, pp. 125–29.

23. *Parents* magazine, for AP Special Features, "New Dimensions 3–6; Parents Rank Violence As Top Worry in New Nationwide Survey," Associated Press, 6 March 2000.

24. Cathleen Decker, "Finding Quality Child Care a Tough Task," *Los Angeles Times,* 20 June 1999, p. A1.

25. Marilyn Gardner, "Parents Speak: Home Care Is Way Better Than Day Care," *Christian Science Monitor,* 23 August 2000, p. 2.

26. U.S. Census Bureau report, December 2001.

27. 1995 study by Families and Work Institute, cited in Sylvia Ann Hewlett and Cornel West, *The War against Parents* (Boston: Houghton Mifflin, 1998), p. 107.

28. Claudia Shuster, "Employed First-Time Mothers: A Typology of Maternal Responses to Integrating Parenting and Employment," *Family Relations* 4 (1993), pp. 13–20.

29. G. K. Chesterton, *All Things Considered* (London: Cox & Wyman Ltd., 1908), p. 70.

30. Jennifer Roback Morse, "Why the Market Can't Raise Our Children for Us," *American Enterprise,* May/June 1998, p. 56.

31. "Factors Change Child Rearing," Associated Press, 22 May 2002.

32. Kay Hymowitz, "Fear and Loathing at the Day-Care Center," *City Journal* 11:3 (Summer 2001).

33. Richard Lowry, "Nasty, Brutish, and Short: Children in Day Care—and the Mothers Who Put Them There," *National Review,* 28 May 2001.

34. *Newsweek,* 19 November 1990.

35. Penelope Leach, *Children First: What Our Society Must Do and Is Not Doing for Our Children* (New York: Alfred Knopf, 1994), p. 22.

36. Interview with Senator Christopher Dodd during Hearing of the Subcommittee on Children, Families, Drugs, and Alcoholism of the Senate Committee on Human Resources, 100th Congress, 2nd Session, 28 June 1988.

37. Luncheon Discussion at Brookings National Issues Forum on "Creating a Better Start for Children: A New Look at Child Care and Early Childhood Education," 21 April 1999, Federal News Service transcript.

38. Anne Morse, "Not So Swift," *World,* 30 June 2001, p. 37.

Six: The Family under Siege

1. Karl Zinsmeister, "The Problem with Day Care," *American Enterprise,* May/June 1998, pp. 29–31.

2. Ibid.

3. Ibid, p. 37.

4. Ibid.

5. Interview with Dr. Brenda Hunter, *Beverly LaHaye Live,* 11 February 1998.

6. Stanley I. Greenspan, unpublished manuscript, quoted in Charmaine Crouse Yoest, "Behind the Push for Day Care," *Family Policy* 11:1 (March 1998).

7. Bryce Christensen, ed., *Day Care: Child Psychology and Adult Economics* (Rockford, Illinois: Rockford Institute, 1989), p. vii.

8. Bruno Bettelheim, *The Children of the Dream* (New York: Avon, 1970).

9. David Brooks, "The Organization Kid," *Atlantic Monthly,* April 2001.

10. David Elkind, *The Hurried Child: Growing Up Too Fast Too Soon* (New York: Perseus, 2001).

11. John Bruer, *The Myth of the First Three Years* (New York: The Free Press, 1999).

12. Quoted in Kay Hymowitz, "Fear and Loathing at the Day-Care Center," *City Journal* 11:3 (Summer 2001), pp. 58–67.

13. Ibid.

14. Clifford Cobb, Ted Halstead and Jonathan Rowe, "If the GDP Is Up, Why Is America Down?" *Atlantic Monthly,* October 1995, p. 66.

15. Christopher Lasch, preface to Charles Siegel, *What's Wrong with Day Care* (New York: Teachers' College Press, 2001), p. vii.

16. William D. Gairdner, *The War against Parents* (Toronto: Stoddart Publishing, 1992), p. 335.

17. Ibid.

18. Lasch, preface to Siegel, *What's Wrong with Day Care,* p. x.

19. See Brian Robertson, *There's No Place Like Work* (Dallas: Spence, 2000), pp. 33–74.

20. Margaret O'Brien Steinfels, *Who's Minding the Children?* (New York: Simon & Schuster, 1973), pp. 62–63.

21. Linda Greenhouse, "Panel in Senate Starts Hearings on Child Care," *New York Times,* 13 June 1987, p. 26.

22. G. K. Chesterton, *What's Wrong with the World* (New York: Dodd, Mead & Co., 1910), p. 170.

23. Allan Carlson "The New Child Abuse: Two Case-Studies of Wrong-Headed Public Policy," *The Family in America,* July 1998.

24. Zinsmeister, "The Problem with Day Care," p. 28.

25. CWA Library (cwfa.org), "Whose Hand Should Rock the Cradle?" (20 May 1998),p. 4.

26. Dale O'Leary, *The Gender Agenda* (Lafayette, Indiana: Vital Issues Press, 1997) p. 136.

27. Ibid.

28. Gairdner, *The War against Parents,* p. 335.

29. CWA, "Whose Hand Should Rock the Cradle?" p. 8.

30. Dana Mack, *The Assault on Parenthood* (New York: Simon & Schuster, 1997), p. 166.

31. Ibid., p. 173.

32. "Creating a Better Start for Children: A New Look at Child Care and Early Childhood Education," a Brookings National Issues Forum, 21 April 1999, transcript by Federal News Service, Washington, D.C.

33. E. Belle Evans and George E. Saia, *Day Care for Infants: The Case for Infant Day Care and a Practical Guide* (Boston: Beacon Press, 1972), p. 6.

34. Emily Eakin, "Did Cradles Always Rock? Or Did Mom Once Not Care?" *New York Times,* 30 June 2001, p. B7.

35. Susan Caba, "She Loves Me, She Loves Me Not," *Hamilton Spectator,* 10 December 1999, p. A13.

36. Stanley I. Greenspan, M.D., *The Four-Thirds Solution: Solving the Child-Care Crisis in America Today* (Cambridge, Massachusetts: Perseus Publishing, 2001), p. 10.

37. Allan Carlson, "Corporate America and the Family," *Family Policy* 14:6 (November/December 2001).

38. Ibid.

39. Ibid.

40. Ibid.

41. David Wagner, "Turning Hearts towards the Office," *Insight, 22* July 1996, p. 3.

42. Christopher Lasch, *Women and the Common Life* (New York, W. W. Norton & Co., 1997), pp. 118–19.

43. Ibid., p. 6.

44. Siegel, *What's Wrong with Day Care,* p. 90.

Seven: How Parents Can Take Back Parenting

1. *Day Care: Scientific and Social Policy Issues,* ed. Edward F. Zigler and Edmund W. Gordon (Boston: Auburn House Publishing Co., 1982), pp. 260–63.

2. Maggie Gallagher, "Bush Advisor's Not-So-Secret Weapon: More Work for Wives," Universal Press Syndicate, 29 March 2000.

3. Gail Collins, "A Mommy Track Derails," *New York Times,* 11 January 2000, op-ed page.

4. Michael Ellison, *The Guardian,* 3 September 2001.

5. David H. Ciscel, David C. Sharp and Julia A. Heath, "Family Work Trends and Practices: 1971 to 1991," *Journal of Family and Economic Issues* 21:1 (Spring 2000), pp. 23–36.

6. Sar A. Levitan, Richard S. Belus and Frank Gallo, *What's Happening to the American Family?* (Baltimore: Johns Hopkins University Press, 1988), p. 131.

7. Charles Siegel, *What's Wrong with Day Care* (New York: Teachers' College Press, 2001), p. 88.

8. Kristin Smith, *Who's Minding the Kids? Child Care Arrangements: Spring 1997*, U.S. Census Bureau, Current Population Reports, July 2002.

9. Scott Hodge, Heritage Foundation Fellow, interview by Concerned Women for America, May 1997.

10. Allan Carlson and David Hartman, "How the Tax Code Discriminates against the Traditional Family," Institute for Policy Innovation, 12 February 2002.

11. William R. Prosser and Sharon M. McGroder, "The Supply and Demand for Child Care: Measurement and Analytic Issues," in *Child Care in the 1990s: Trends and Consequences,* ed. Alan Booth (Hillsdale, New Jersey: Lawrence Erlbaum Associates, 1992), p. 47.

12. Michael Schwartz, "The Simplest Solution Is the Best," *Family Affairs* 2:1 (Spring 1989), published by the Institute for American Values.

13. Robert Rector, "Fourteen Myths about Families and Child Care," *Harvard Journal on Legislation* 26:517, p. 525.

14. Richard T. Gill, "Day Care or Personal Care?" *Public Interest,* Fall 1991.

15. Siegel, *What's Wrong with Day Care,* p. 69.

16. "Stand up if You Would Rather Be Raised by a Daycare Worker," interview with Dr. Laura Schlessinger, *Human Events,* 18 June 2001, p. 13.

Index